SILENT QUARTERBACK

THE SAM COPPOLA STORY

A TRUE STORY OF
EVERY MAN'S DREAM

By Sam Coppola

As told to Rick Osbourne

Copyright Notices

Published under the Copyright Laws of the Library Of Congress of The United States of America, by:

PYOW Publishing
21W280 Coronet Rd.
Lombard, IL 60148
Telephone 630-495-3445

International Standard Book Number (ISBN), 978-0-9766965-9-9

Cover by Pam and Cody Osbourne
Illustrations by Betty Baker

This book is dedicated to...

Tom Uva, my great friend after whom my second son Tommy was named.

Dick Mollo, my great friend who was the wind beneath my wings when it came to organizing and promoting the Sam Coppola Baseball League.

Al Fenaroli, my great friend and roommate at Fordham University...a player and a man I'll never forget.

Al Shanen, my great friend, coach of the Stamford Golden Bears. Al was the finest football mind I ever encountered.

Charles Magyar, my great friend and the man who pushed and pushed until I finally wrote this book.

Jo Jo and Mike, My older brother (JoJo) and my younger brother (Mike) who were both major influences in my life, in two very different ways.

Millie and my Kids – This book would never have been possible because my life would have been infinitely different had it not been for Millie and my kids. I have been blessed. Everyone should be so lucky.

Foreward

I am honored to be asked to write the forward to this book on the life of Sam Coppola, a personal friend for more years than I can recall---and his football coach when he played for the Stamford Golden Bears.

If legends are born or made, he is both. Sam came from a humble background, born on the West Side of Stamford, Connecticut and became that legend: husband, father, caretaker of his special-needs brother, developer, tile worker, business owner, outstanding football and baseball player—a true Renaissance man.

In life timing is so important. At a different time and place, Sam would have been selected by one of the teams in the fledging A.F.L., or even with the established N.F.L. But, instead, he gained greatness with a semi-pro team called the Stamford Golden Bears, a team that produced several players that were picked up by the N.F.L. teams, two, Alan Webb and Johnnie Counts, by the New York Giants.

Sam should have been selected by an N.F.L. team. He had all the ability and attributes to make it in the pros. Sam had "quick feet, a quick release, was exceptionally physical and durable"—the four main assets for a pro quarterback. Sam was an early version of Brett Favre.

On the field, he knew how to take chances, run plays that were not in the playbook, find the open man, and somehow he found a way to win.

It's about a time, a place, a kind of game, a man we will never see again.   Life has its disappointments. He was overlooked. I think you will find this human-interest story of Sam Coppola compelling. A story like this is not uncommon. He just needed that one shot at fame, but it never came!!! If it had, he would have made it in the NFL.

Coach Al Shanen

Contents

The 90 MPH Fastball

"Regrets, I have a few, but then again, too few to mention."
Frank Sinatra, "My Way"

When he was fifteen years old (1945) Sam Coppola had a 90 mph fastball and an opportunity to try out with the World Champion Brooklyn Dodgers. His father drove him to the legendary Ebbets Field where renowned players like Jackie Robinson, Duke Snyder, Roy Campanella, Pee Wee Reese, Johnny Podres, Don Newcomb, Don Drysdale, and Sandy Koufax played and made baseball history.

In the locker room, Sam was handed a full uniform along with an invitation to show his stuff on the mound. He did so and the scouts informed Sam and his dad that they'd be back in contact once he graduated from high school.

When he was 17 Sam still had a 90 mph fastball and an opportunity to try out with the Philadelphia Athletics (now the Oakland Athletics). When asked what position he played he told the scouts that he pitched and played third base, but he preferred playing third over pitching, so he took batting practice and grounders instead of a turn on the pitching mound. In the process Sam passed up a golden opportunity to spotlight his blazing fastball.

Looking back on these incidents, along with many others like them, the question for Sam Coppola, now age 79, retired and living in Boca Raton, FL is not *"Did I have all the tools to make it in the pros?"* The question that's haunting him, gnawing at him at this point in his life is, *"Since I had all the tools, why didn't I make it in the pros?"*

Sam at Ebbets Field at age 15

Sam, age 15, on the mound at Ebbets Field

Coppola Lived an Exemplary Life, But...

To be sure, this was not a "successful life vs. an unsuccessful life" kind of question. By all standards Sam Coppola lived a full and exemplary life and had disappointed no-one with his 79 bountiful years of living.

Born at the beginning of the Great Depression (July 23, 1930) to an Italian, working class family, Coppola grew up on the streets of Stamford, CT, graduated from high school and college (Fordham University). He spent a couple of years in the Marine Corps, was discharged and returned home to oversee the family business. Then he got married, raised a happy and healthy family, and by the time retirement came along he'd saved enough money for he and his wife Millie to retire comfortably in Boca Raton, FL.

The Voice Inside His Head

Regardless of the trappings though, there was still this small voice in the back closet of Sam's mind that kept the question burning brightly… a flame that simply refused to be extinguished. Like his father before him, he loved sports. But unlike his father before him, Sam also played sports with an astonishing degree of success unknown to his peers.

In elementary and junior high school, Sam was inevitably the first one chosen when the kids picked sides for anything. At age 15 he could throw a baseball 90 miles per hour, and a football 65 yards standing flat footed…with accuracy. In high school he lettered in four sports including baseball, football, basketball, and track.

After high school he was recruited to play football by a number of colleges including Princeton, Rutgers, Georgia, and Fordham University. After college Sam joined the Marines where he won the starting quarterback position over several highly regarded, former college quarterbacks.

And when he was discharged from the Marines and returned home to oversee Stamford Tile, Inc. (the family business) he was recruited by the Stamford Golden Bears of the Atlantic Coast Football Conference where he annually led the league in passing for over a decade.

In short, Sam Coppola had all the tools to make it in the NFL, so why didn't he make it? That's the question that pops into his mind when he watches the modern day professional football heroes being paid multi-millions, placed on pedestals, and deified by a public that can't seem to get enough of what they do on and off of the football field. It's also the question that animates the remainder of this book from back in the shadows… like a flame that refuses to die.

On the Streets of Stamford, CT

In the early years Sam recalls his father, Michael, buying and running a tavern in the wake of Prohibition's repeal in 1933, while running a tile business on the side.

"My father was a workaholic who worked seven days a week including the holidays," Sam said. "When he sold the tavern and went full time with Stamford Tile, Inc., his schedule didn't change very much. But we were always a tight knit Italian family who looked out for each other. And on the holidays we always waited until my dad got home before digging into the lasagna or the ravioli, which was our traditional holiday meal back then."

Poor? According to Whom?

By today's standards the Coppola family was poor and had to scrape for everything they had. By the same token the Great Depression was an equal opportunity destroyer of opportunity, so Sam and his brothers Joseph and Michael Jr. never felt poor or underprivileged because everyone they knew was in the same boat.

"Every once in a while my father would take us to Yankee Stadium see a major league baseball game and it seemed like they always cracked a bat or two. Mike and I begged him to let us take the broken bats home where we could nail and tape them together and play with them for months if not years. And hand me down mitts were the rule not the exception in our neighborhood. But that didn't stop us from learning to hit, throw, and field a baseball just like the major leaguers we read about in the Stamford Advocate."

For the Love of Sports

The Coppola boys loved sports and they practiced hard in order to become as good as they could be. More often than not, the regular practice transformed them into winners of their 3 on 3 under the lights football games on Spruce Street in Stamford, CT back in the late 30's.

"We always despised sitting around doing nothing and being bored to death. And sports was our antidote to nothingness and to boredom," Sam said. "We'd walk two miles from our house on Spruce Street to Woodside Park in order to play a baseball game with a group of kids who called themselves the Stillwater Indians."

Other groups of kids came on board so one day Sam decided they needed to create a schedule so they'd know who and when they were playing. This took them out of the pick-up phase and into an informal league.

The Coppola Brothers

Sam's brother Joseph (JoJo) was two years older and born with a disability. Mentally, Jo never grew beyond the age of six years, didn't attend school, and never learned to read or write. Michael, on the other hand, was a younger version of Sam in terms of his athletic ability and prowess.

"Because of his limitations, Michael and I always felt like JoJo was our kid brother. Wherever he went, everyone loved him and everyone looked out for him. He often went to work with my father at Stamford Tile, which gave him a sense of self confidence, and at the same time it earned him a little spending money. JoJo always wanted to have a job just like everyone else in the family, and my dad was the one who made sure that he had one."

Sam and Michael would also take Joseph to the corner tavern, the neighborhood gathering place, where everyone knew that orange soda was his favorite drink. The regular customers inevitably kept his glass full of orange soda while JoJo loved every second of it.

The presence of Joseph gave Sam and Michael a sense of humility and empathy for the underdog that they may not have felt had it not been for their older brother. In other words it would have been easy for natural athletes like Sam and Michael to let things go to their heads. Joseph prevented that from happening. The fact that Sam identified and empathized with the underdog throughout his life had everything to do with JoJo's influence.

Michael Jr., on the other hand could physically fend for himself. After graduating from high school Michael played six seasons worth of minor league baseball in the Kansas City A's (now Oakland A's) organization.

"Mike had forearms like Arnold Palmer or Popeye," said Sam. "And he could hit a baseball further than any human I've ever known. During his six year minor league career, Mike hit over 200 home runs, and he set the single season mark in the Appalachian League with 39 home runs in 1956. Then one day he decided that he was tired of all the travel, he retired from baseball, went home, got married, and took a position in Stamford Tile where he worked for 43 years before he finally retired in 1999."

Michael Senior, the Workaholic

Michael Sr. was the workaholic role model for all the boys. Work was imbedded into the DNA of Sam and Michael Jr., both of whom fully understood that if you wanted something, you'd better be willing to earn it.

"It was undoubtedly my dad's influence that made us work as hard as we did at sports," said Sam. "I never missed a practice in my entire life. In fact I usually showed up early and left late. I wanted to make sure that nobody ever out-worked me. More than anything else that's probably why I was successful in sports. I worked at being good every day, every week, every month, all year long," he added. "I always found that the harder I worked, the easier the game became."

Eva, Whatever Her Boys Needed

Eva, Sam's mom was a worker as well. In an age when most moms were not working outside the house, Eva was putting in 20 to 30 hours a week at the Clairol factory in order to make sure her three boys had everything they needed to grow up strong and independent.

"She was also a great cook, and a caring mother who had a special challenge on her plate with JoJo always under her wing," said Sam. "The biggest thing Mike and I learned from our parents was to never be afraid to work at those things that are really important to you. That's how you get good at anything – you work at it," he added.

Sam's First Formal Taste of Sporting Success

Sam's first formal sporting experience came when he tried out for the boxing team at Cloonan Junior High. At 5'10", 130 pounds, he'd never donned a pair of boxing gloves in his life when he went in to see Coach Goldberg to say he wanted to try out for the team.

First Sam made the Cloonan School team. Then he won Cloonan's 130 pound division. Cloonan then went on to compete as a team at the city level where Sam prevailed once again and became 130 lb boxing champ of Stamford, CT in 1944 at age 14.

"I was so proud of winning the championship that I wore the medal to school the next morning and some of the kids laughed at me. But their laughing didn't faze me. I'd won the title and I was so proud that nothing they could say or do would have made any difference," Sam said. It was the first and last time Sam ever entered a boxing ring.

Young Sam Coppola working out on the heavy bag.

The Sporting Seed Begins to Grow

From this point forward the sporting seed just grew larger and larger until it became who Sam Coppola was, and how he was identified at St Basil High. His favorite sports were football and baseball. But since the coaches wanted him to stay in shape during the off season, Sam was expected to go out for basketball and track and field as well, which he did and he proceeded to letter in all four sports.

In his junior year Sam transferred to Eastern Military Academy where he was elected captain of the football team, led the conference in passing, and was named the most valuable athlete in school. College and university scouts began showing interest in the young athlete. But when they got a look at his grades they backed away and Coppola knew he had to mend his ways if he was going to attend college on an athletic scholarship as he'd planned to do.

"I put all my eggs in the athletic basket and almost none into the academic basket," said Sam. "As I've said previously, if you don't work at it, don't expect to be good at it. I wasn't a good student and that had to change."

Sam accepts the "best all around athlete trophy" from Coach Murphy

Sam Makes a Promise

When his senior year rolled around Coach Murphy approached Sam and his dad with the news that he'd accepted a new job at rival school Carteret Prep, in West Orange, NJ, and the athletic director requested that Murphy bring his star football player along with him. If he did, they'd offer Sam a full scholarship so it wouldn't cost a dime for him to attend.

In order to win his father's approval Sam promised that he'd buckle down and study. Michael Sr. agreed to Coach Murphy's request and Sam transferred to Carteret.

"Nobody in our family had ever attended college before," said Sam. "So I could be the first to attend and graduate from college, but only if I got my grades up and was accepted into the schools that were recruiting me. I knew I had to become more than just another jock. I began studying for the first time in my life"

At Carteret Prep, Coppola had another stellar year on the football field, was elected team captain, was conference passing champ, and an All Conference team-member. Once again he lettered in all four sports, but this year he spent hours every night pouring over textbooks that had meant so little in previous years. Sam Coppola took the bull by the horns and made it his business to become more than just another jock. For the first time ever, Sam became a student.

Carteret Prep Student Council President

Much to his surprise, a number of his friends, and several teachers suggested that Sam run for Student Council President. It was an even bigger surprise when this now "student athlete" was elected Student Council President at Carteret Prep. "I'd never done anything like this in my entire life, but when I won, I decided to give it 100% and I had a wonderful year at Carteret," said Sam.

Sam is the guy seated…in the center

With his athletic prowess in hand and his new found grades, letters from college football coaches began pouring in from around the country. "With the help of Coach Murphy we narrowed the choices down to Rutgers, who promised to make a T-formation quarterback out of me if I attended school there, and Fordham who was a perennial football powerhouse back in those years."

Fordham University

In the end, Coppola chose to attend Fordham because of their schedule. He was offered a full, all expense paid, unconditional athletic scholarship. "That basically meant that if you were injured and unable to play any more, the scholarship stayed intact. They couldn't take it away. "

When he arrived on campus in the fall of 1950 Sam discovered that Fordham's coach was planning to play him at offensive and defensive halfback instead of quarterback.

Naturally shy and wanting to avoid conflict with his new coaches, Sam played the positions he was asked to play without complaining, and he became a standout football player at Fordham. However during four full years of college football, he didn't take a single snap as a quarterback, the position he was naturally built to play.

Al Fenaroli

Sam's roommate during his freshman year was a very talented, 6' 2"', 250 pound offensive tackle named Al Fenaroli whose specialty was whipping Fordham's senior linemen on a regular basis. But since freshman were ineligible to play at the varsity level back then, Fenaroli and Sam both spent year one with playing on the freshman squad.

"As it turned out Al had a younger sister who had the same kinds of challenges as my brother Jo. And he was as tuned into her as I was into JoJo. Because of our experiences in this regard, Al and I became best friends at Fordham, and we've kept track of each other ever since."

Defensive Guard?

During his senior year, in a game at Quantico, VA against the Quantico Marines, Sam was playing offensive halfback, and he was sitting on the bench waiting for his team to get the ball back when a defensive guard became injured and had to be taken out of the game. Thin on defensive lineman, his coach approached Sam and asked him to fill in at defensive guard for the remainder of the game.

"At 6', 185 pounds, I played the entire game at offensive halfback, and over half the game at defensive guard," Sam said. "When the game was over Coach DeFilippo came up and told me that I'd played a hell of a game. It was the greatest compliment he ever paid me. "

Call Me the Silent Quarterback

"To this day I don't think he ever knew that I'd come to Fordham to play quarterback. So for four years I failed to open my mouth and tell Coach DeFilippo because I wasn't a boat rocker. Not only that, but the college diploma was the main reason I was attending Fordham and I didn't want to risk graduation. Call me the silent quarterback," Sam said.

The Marines

In 1953 Sam graduated from Fordham and his buddy Al Fenaroli was named the valedictorian of the class. With the Korean conflict winding down Sam joined the Marines spending one year in El Toro, CA where he played over 80 baseball games, and another year in Honolulu, HI where he played a whole lot of football.

Hearing that Coppola had been a football star at Fordham, his commanding officer Colonel Sweetser asked Sam to try out for the Marine's football team on the island. He'd just finished playing an 80 plus game baseball season and he told the Colonel that he was hoping to get a little rest. But the Colonel thought Sam could help his football team so he offered Sam a staff car and time off if he'd just give it a try. Sam agreed, and the next morning he drove the car across the island where tryouts were being held.

"When I arrived they gave me a full uniform and the coach asked what position I played in college. I thought twice and finally said that I was a quarterback. Knowing there were several highly regarded, former college quarterbacks in the running, I figured I'd have no chance and would be sent back to my squad across the island."

"We practiced for three days and at the end the last day the coach came up and announced that Sam Coppola was his starting quarterback. I was astonished, but I have to admit that it was like riding a bike. Everything just came back to me as if I'd been playing quarterback the past four years at Fordham," Coppola said.

The league included teams from the Marine Corps, the Navy, the Army, a couple of local semi-pro teams, and the University of Hawaii which was unable to do much traveling, and lacked competition back in those days. Taking up where he'd left off four years before, Sam led the Island League in passing, was the league MVP, and won nine consecutive games before injury struck early in the first quarter during the tenth and final game against University of Hawaii.

The Strange Proposition

A couple hours before the game Sam was getting his morning rub down from a local masseur when this fellow suggested that he could make it worth Sam's time and effort if he'd throw a pass or two into the dirt in order to enhance a couple of bets that he'd made the day before.

"I sat straight up, grabbed the guy by his shirt collar, pushed him up against the wall and told him in no uncertain terms that if he ever said anything like that to me again he'd regret it. Then I got dressed to play without giving the incident another thought," Coppola said.

The Coincidental Injury

Early in the first quarter his protection was breaking down so Sam ran a bootleg to the right side of the field when a defensive back tackled him directly on the left knee. "I felt it buckle. I went down to the ground and was unable to get back up. They brought the stretcher out, took me to the hospital and informed me that the bruising was bad enough that they couldn't operate for several days. They finally operated, and as it turned out, I spent at least six weeks in rehab where I was advised I might never play football again. Needless to say, the tools I thought could lead to the NFL were now in jeopardy. "

In that final game however, the Marines were favored by 28 points at kickoff. But with their captain, quarterback, and team leader in the hospital with his leg in traction, the Marines lost 34 to 17 to the underdogs from the University of Hawaii and finished the season 9 and 1 instead of 10 and 0. "When the game was over I was more than a little disappointed because if I had avoided the injury, I'm sure we could have won that game," Sam said.

The First Ever Hula Bowl Game

In the wake of the final game an All Star Team was chosen that included five NFL players who were currently on active duty in Hawaii, and Sam Coppola was named the starting quarterback. They were scheduled to play the first ever Hula Bowl against a group of College All Stars from the states. But with his entire leg in a cast Coppola was so disappointed that he couldn't bring himself to even watch the game. With his discharge looming on the immediate horizon, Sam knew it was time to move on.

Home Run Number 39

In late 1956 Sam was discharged from the Marines. He flew to Los Angeles, rented a car from Hertz, and drove cross country to Wytheville, VA where brother Mike was playing minor league baseball in the Kansas City A's organization and was threatening to break the Appalachian League's home run record of 38. Sam wanted to have a front row seat when Mike hammered home run number 39.

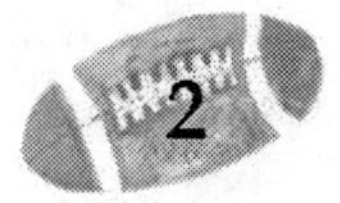

Family Business vs. Professional Sports

"Twenty years from now you'll be more disappointed in the things you didn't do than the things you did do. So throw off the bow lines, sail away from the safe harbor, catch the trade winds in your sails and explore, dream, discover." **Mark Twain**

In August of 1956, when Sam Coppola's plane touched down in Los Angles, Elvis Presley's "You Ain't Nothing But a Hound Dog" was at the top of the Billboard charts, people were watching The Lone Ranger, Ed Sullivan, American Bandstand, and Ozzie and Harriet on small black and white TV screens. The world had yet to hear of JFK and Jackie, Muhammad Ali, Joe Namath, the Beatles or the Rolling Stones. WW II hero Dwight David (Ike) Eisenhower was President, and construction on America's Interstate Highway System had yet to begin.

So what did all this have to do with the recently discharged Marine who'd just rented a Chevy from Hertz in order to travel cross country to see his brother Mike break the Appalachian League home run record? It meant that 2700 miles worth of two lane highway, complete with slow moving trucks, stretched between Sam and his Wytheville, VA destination. Driving 10 hours a day, (no Cruise Control or GPS in '56) Sam left on a Monday morning and arrived in Wytheville late Thursday afternoon, ready to *watch* his brother for a few games before heading home to Stamford.

During his previous five seasons of minor league ball Mike had already hit over 170 home runs and in this, his sixth season, he was having his best year ever at the plate. As a matter of fact, when Sam arrived in early August Mike had already hit 36 homers and was sneaking up on the Appalachian League record of 38. Sam vowed to stay in Virginia until his brother Mike broke the record.

Watching VS Playing Minor League Baseball

Much to his surprise, Sam's baseball reputation had preceded him, so instead of sitting in the stands and eating hot dogs, he was asked to try out for the team. He not only tried out, but he made the team, played left field, and hit over 300 for the Wytheville Athletics (double A farm team of the Kansas City Athletics who now reside in Oakland, CA) until the 1956 season was finally over. And, during those last three weeks of the season Mike successfully knocked out homers number 37, 38, and 39…all of which Sam witnessed first hand while sitting on the bench instead of in the stands.

"That was not only a thrill for Mike, but it was a thrill for me just to be there," Sam said. For three straight weeks the Coppola brothers lit up the diamond together for the Wytheville, VA Athletics. But that didn't stop Mike from dropping a bomb shell on Sam when the season was over.

"Playing on the team instead of watching Mike play was surprise number one for Sam. Surprise number two was when Mike announced that he was tired of playing minor league baseball, all the travel, and all the hotels.

"Mike told me he was going to retire, come home, work for Stamford Tile and to help my father and I build the business." With that stunning piece of news, Sam climbed into Mike's hot pink Ford T-Bird with which the A's management had lured him into signing six years ago and they drove home together.

Stamford Tile's Chief Cook and Bottle Washer

By 1956 Mike Senior had been running Stamford Tile, Inc. with a small staff, for a decade and a half…ever since he sold the tavern in 1936. During those initial years it was Mike

Senior who worked 10 and 12 hours a day, at least six days a week. It was Mike Senior who ordered the supplies, sold the jobs, oversaw the jobs, and collected the receivables. He was the quintessential chief cook and bottle washer, and because he was covering so many bases himself, the business grew very little in its first decade and a half.

Mike Jr. Retires From Baseball

With Sam and Michael now on board the opportunity to grow Stamford Tile had finally presented itself, but not without a few questions being asked up front.

"At first my father didn't understand why I wanted to work for Stamford Tile instead of some big corporation in New York City. After all, I was the first person in the family with a college degree. I'd graduated from Fordham's business department. He wanted to know why I wanted to work in this small business where I'd have to wear all hats, instead of wearing a white collar, a tie, and carrying a briefcase somewhere in Manhattan?"

Captain of His Own Ship

Sam explained that although Stamford Tile was currently small, he thought there was some terrific growth potential sitting right out on the horizon if they were ready to make it happen. Not only that, Mike Senior had always been the boy's role model and had always been his own boss instead of working for someone else. Just like his dad, Sam also aspired to be the captain of his own ship and he knew that Stamford Tile offered an opportunity that he may never have in a giant Wall Street corporation.

So instead of playing executive in a high rise office building on the Avenue of the Americas, and climbing a corporate ladder, Sam took over Stamford Tile's books from Eva, his mother who'd been overseeing the numbers ever since the company started a decade and a half ago.

He and brother Mike also sold and oversaw jobs (i.e. projects), mixed cement, and tiled bathrooms in Stamford residences from one side of Fairfield County to the other. Sam often ended the day with dirt under his fingernails, which would never have happened if he'd chosen the corporate option. He was indeed a unique mixture of white and blue collar as he and Mike worked their way into the business. And grow it they did, in ways that could never have happened previously.

Once an Athlete, Always an Athlete

But in his heart of hearts Sam Coppola was an athlete first and a businessman second. Yes, he wanted to grow Stamford Tile with his brother Mike. But unlike Mike, Sam still had this yearning for the game – particularly the game of football.

Soon after he returned to Stamford Sam was approached by his cousin Mike Potenza and his partner Dennis (Whitey) Behunick who owned the Stamford Golden Bears, a local semi-pro football team.

Mike Potenza, all New York-Connecticut League tackle, and Denny Behunick, operators of the Golden Bears football squad, have announced a policy to book heavy independent football clubs to augment the Bears' schedule in league play. The first major independent foe will be the Jersey City Vikings, Sept. 27. The Staten

Mike Potenza and Denny (Whitey) Behunick

"Mike knew about my quarterbacking success in high school and in the Marines. I said I'd sign if Coach Shanen would make me his quarterback. He answered by sliding the contract over, and motioning for me to sign." Thus began a 10 year semi-pro career (1956-'66) in the Atlantic Coast Football Conference, with three different teams, where Sam Coppola led the league in passing every year that he played.

Ten Hour Days

Ten hour days at Stamford Tile, in addition to a semi pro football career meant that Sam got into the habit of rising early and playing late. "We practiced several times a week under the lights on St. Cecelia School's blacktop parking lot. We wore sneakers instead of cleats. But the fact that we practiced at night and played mostly on Saturday evenings under the lights, or Sunday afternoons allowed me to squeeze football into my life," Sam said. "And I don't remember ever missing a practice. In fact I usually showed up early and stayed late so the receivers and I could polish our precision timing. I just loved playing the game."

They Played on High School Fields

All games were played on local high school fields, including their home games which were played on Stamford High's home field, one of the best football facilities on the east coast back then. When they arrived at the field the players all suited up and took warm ups, Sam throwing, backs catching and running, and linemen doing a variety of blocking and tackling drills to make sure they were ready to play.

Football Had Yet to Become a Big Business

"Back then helmets had a single bar face mask," Sam said. "It was just enough for a defensive lineman or back to grab hold and twist my neck off, which happened on more than one occasion. Our shoes had cleats that screwed on and off. Back in those days football had yet to become a big business, and the equipment reflected the times," he added.

Love and Marriage

In August of 1958 Sam thought he'd fallen in love so he married a Stamford girl by the name of Barbara Miller. They'd known each other since high school, and both thought they were ready to settle down and raise a family. Within the first year Barbara became pregnant. On July 27 of 1959 his baby daughter Tracy was born, and Sam Coppola became a father for the first time.

"But 10 and 12 hour work days, along with evening football (and baseball) practices, with games on the weekends left little time to cultivate a marriage. After two years we divorced and went our separate ways," Sam said.

Several months later Sam was introduced to a pretty young brown eyed beauty named Millie House. The attraction was immediate and mutual. Sam was the local super-star athlete, and Millie the young lady who had just moved in town from Rumford, Maine a little town located about 500 miles northeast of Stamford. Sam and Millie seemed to be a match that had destiny written all over it.

Millie had been raised in a family in which both parents put in long and active days. That is to say, the Coppola's "constant motion orientation to life" was already familiar to Millie. After two years of dating they married in 1963 and proceeded to maintain the rapid fire pace for another two years before having their first child in 1965.

Growing the Family Business

For five years Sam, Mike Jr., and Mike Sr. concentrated on growing Stamford Tile. "Michael Sr. always took great pride in his work which inevitably generated lots of referrals, said Sam. "In other words, my father grew the business with lots of word of mouth advertising, which is how you do it when you don't have a lot of money to start with."

"Mike Jr. and I maintained the tradition of quality workmanship and we also started running some Yellow Page ads, as well as some newspaper ads, and even a TV spot or two on occasion. With three of us now in the business we also started wholesaling to other contractors in and around the area. We were really on a roll," said Sam.

Tragedy Strikes

Then in 1961, tragedy struck. Mike Sr., the 52 year old, workaholic and captain of the Coppola's ship seemed to be losing a little energy. Late in the summer he developed a pain in his right elbow that bothered him so much that he finally gave in and consented to paying the doctor a visit.

Now Mike Sr. was a guy who took pride in being so healthy that he'd successfully avoided doctors for years. This was a clear sign that the elbow was really bothering him. Dr. Namoint diagnosed the problem as a severe case of bursitis and he gave Mike Sr. a prescription to relieve the pain.

"The next morning I heard a knock at the door. When I answered my friend Charlie Rosa looked me straight in the eyes, took a deep breath, and proceeded to tell me that my dad had experienced a massive heart attack and passed away," said Sam. "I was speechless and collapsed in a heap on the floor. Charlie picked me up, put one of my arms over his shoulder and helped me out to his car. By the time we arrived at the house Mike Jr. and Joseph were there and we all comforted Mom as best we could."

The Silent Quarterback Takes Charge

In a state of disarray, Sam automatically took charge and made arrangements for the wake and the funeral. The news of Michael Coppola's passing as posted in the Stamford Advocate drew lots of attention. Friends, acquaintances, and business associates paid their respects to a man who was known and respected throughout the area.

Michael Sr. was one of those guys who'd never had a sick day in his life. He was physically active and fit at age 52, so his passing caught everyone by surprise, especially his wife Eva. It also left Eva in a particularly vulnerable position with Joseph who was fully grown, but mentally functioned on the level of a six year old. Joseph was totally dependent on his parents, one of which was now suddenly gone forever.

As was his habit Sam stepped up to the plate in order to fill the void. He took over the reins of the family business by becoming President and CEO of Stamford Tile in the midst of a growth spurt. He and Millie took over the big, three story house in which the Coppola's had all grown up. With the money he'd made from his dad's insightful and timely investment, they bought a beautiful, 3 BR house for Ma Coppola and JoJo, and Sam put his mother on full salary so she and Joseph would have no financial concerns.

Sam also made sure that all JoJo's bases were covered as well. "He was like my kid brother, even though he was two years older than me," Sam said. "We tried our best to fill the void that my dad's passing created, but to be honest we all struggled for a while. Eventually we reconciled with it, each in our own way, while my mother lived for another 30 years before she passed in 1993. Joseph hung in there until 2003 when he passed away at age 75."

"But while Ma and Jo were with us, we all made it a practice to visit several times a week. We helped Mom with things around the house, and took her to the grocery store. We kept JoJo in orange soda, made sure that his TV was in good working order. His favorite shows were the Three Stooges, Roy Rogers, and the Lone Ranger, and he loved to talk about them when ever we came over to visit," said Sam.

Adventures in Real Estate

Six months before the loss of Mike Sr., Sam decided he wanted to dabble in some real estate. He spotted a piece of property not too far from Stamford Tile that was for sale. He thought the location was right and that it would be a great place to locate a new apartment complex. Mike Sr. agreed and co-signed for Sam on the land purchase.

In order to avoid allowing any grass to grow beneath his feet, Sam contacted Frank Mercede and Sons, a builder in the area for whom he'd done some tile work. Sam asked if

Mercede would like to partner up on the apartment project. Frank loved the idea. Sam provided the property, Mercede and Sons constructed the building, and suddenly Sam Coppola found himself in the Stamford real estate market.

Serious Money

"Stamford Tile was a good, strong company and Mike Jr. and I were doing real well growing the business. But to be real honest, it wasn't until I started in real estate that I made any serious money. When we sold the apartment complex for example, we made out real well," said Sam.

"And when we'd sell one property we'd always invest in another while the entire thing kind of snowballed in our favor," Sam said. "It made me look like I knew what I was doing with a buck, which I suppose I did. You know it's easy to lose money in real estate, but we didn't. Real estate helped me do some things I'd always wanted to do, and it gave my family some things they'd never have had otherwise."

And a First Time Father

And to complicate matters even more, soon after the apartment complex announced its grand opening, Millie became pregnant. "But with my 10 hour days, Millie decided that she needed to oversee the new 30 unit building," Sam said. "She interviewed all the renters, showed the apartments, collected the rents, and took care of the books all the way up until a week before she went into labor."

"Millie's always has been a trooper and that's one of the big reasons our marriage has succeeded. In lots of ways Millie's like me. We've both always been willing to work hard for the things that we needed and wanted."

In any case, on August 16, 1965 Millie gave birth to an 8 lb, 9 ounce healthy baby boy and Sam became a father for the second time. They named the new baby boy Sam Jr. "To say this was a busy time for us is a gross understatement, at best" Sam said. "We had so many balls in the air at the same time that it was a wonder we survived."

Supply, Demand, and Sam Coppola

So by late 1965 Sam was a new father with a new son. He was a husband with a hard working wife. He was also President and CEO of Stamford Tile, a fast growing business where he spent an average of ten hours a day, while the retail side of the operation, The House of Tile was now being run by Millie and her younger sister Laurel.

He was also taking care of his mother Eva, his brother Joseph, dabbling on real estate on the side, while playing quarterback for the Stamford Golden Bears in the fall, and third base (occasionally pitching) for the Stamford Tilers (the local semi-pro baseball team sponsored by his company) in the summer. During this period of time Sam still had only 24 hours in his day, just like he'd always had. "Sleep," Sam observed "was often pretty hard to come by."

Everybody needed a piece of Sam and he was being pulled in multiple directions by projects and obligations that each had its own unique sense of purpose and meaning. In other words, lightening the load was never one of Sam's options. Nevertheless, he kept on keeping on being the trooper that he'd always been.

But in the Back of His Mind...

But in the back of his mind Sam still felt that he was born to be an athlete. It was the smell of the leather mitt and the feel of two fingers crossing the laces on the baseball that helped him keep it all together in the summer months. And in the fall it was the tight spirals, the cross blocking, the intricate pass routes, and the roar of the crowd collectively rising to its feet when Sam threw another pass into the end zone to one of his speedy wide receivers. For Sam sports had always been the spice of life, that element that made it an adventure, a mountain to climb, an ocean to cross, a reason to be.

In the midst of all this Sam always kept a close eye on the National Football League, Otto Graham, Johnny Unitas, Paul Brown, Y.A. Tittle, Norm Van Brocklin, Willie Galimore, Sam Huff, Big Daddy Lipscomb, Bill George, Paul Hornung, Lennie Moore, Ray Berry, Ollie Matson, and Bobby Lane etc.

Deep in his heart of hearts Sam Coppola longed to quarterback on the big stage, the NFL, where he knew he belonged. He could taste it. He could smell it. He could see himself competing with the best of the best. But for Sam this magical moment remained out there on the horizon, just out of his reach, and to this day he still couldn't explain why.

TV Takes Over Professional Sports

"It's not what you look at that matters. It's what you see."
Henry David Thoreau

In August of 1956 when Sam Coppola returned home from a two year stint in the Marine Corps, the USA was still racially segregated. The family farm that had historically dotted the American landscape still played a very significant role in the nations' economy. And there were thousands of small towns, each with their own schools, churches, banks, libraries, and newspapers from which the local folks got the bulk of their news.

By 1956 however, a seed that had been planted in America's culture prior to WWII had taken root and it was beginning to grow. The seed, known simply as television (TV for short), was destined to change America and the world in ways that not even the most farsighted science fiction speculator could ever have imagined.

Fertile Economic Soil

The technology for TV had been developed at least a decade before WW II broke out, but it wasn't until the troops came home that the seed really began to grow in the fertile economic soil of the 1950's.

By this time, the Great Depression was ancient history. The atomic bomb had put a sudden end to the war. Both supply and demand were growing steadily, which meant that Dad probably had a decent paying job and Mom stayed home and raised the kids.

Under these conditions lots of American citizens could suddenly afford to buy homes (the American dream), automobiles (see the USA in your Chevrolet) washing machines, record players, radios, and yes, television sets.

The Original TV Sets

The original TV's were small by today's standards. The shows of the era included vaudeville personalities like Jack Benny, Milton Berle, George Burns and Gracie Allen; variety shows like the Arthur Godfrey Show, and the Ed Sullivan Hour; sit-coms like the Honeymooners, I Love Lucy, and Ozzie and Harriet; musical shows like The Hit Parade and American Bandstand; and of course westerns like The Lone Ranger, and Roy Rogers.

All of these were viewed in black and white, not in color. The shows themselves were relatively expensive to produce so most programming was created by corporations and syndicated out across the country to an anxiously awaiting, if not adoring audience.

Thus began the homogenization of the American message and culture. People from Stamford, CT to Chicago, Los Angeles, Denver, Omaha and Des Moines were tuned in. Their kids were growing up on the same vicarious experiences, and in the process America's way of viewing the world became increasingly consolidated and homogenized.

Sports Programming

One target that TV programmers concentrated their cameras on during these early years was sporting events that had national appeal. For example, Mel Allen's Friday Night Fights, brought to you by Gillette Blue Blades and White Owl Cigars, became a weekly ritual for men across the nation. In the process, Rocky Marciano, Archie Moore, Jersey Joe Walcott, Kid Gavilan, Ezzard Charles, and Sugar Ray Robinson became nationally recognized celebrities.

Baseball had Dizzy Dean's Game of the Week (featuring Mantle, Maris, Mays, Musial, Ted Williams, etc.). Basketball showcased Bob Cousy, Bill Russell, Bob Pettit, Wilt Chamberlin, and Red Auerbach (along with his famous cigar) in the NBA. And both collegiate and professional football (meaning the NFL), were introduced to the new American spectators in the comfort of their own homes.

In those early years of TV, football fans could watch Jimmy Brown, star fullback for the Cleveland Browns, clash with star linebacker Chuck Bednarik, of the Philadelphia Eagles, or Rick Caseras of the Bears go head on with Ray Nitschke of the Green Bay Packers.

The picture was small, black and white, and it was often fuzzy enough that it was hard to distinguish one player from another. Regardless, a moving picture of an event that was taking place in real time made TV far superior to radio, as more and more American households decided that television was no longer a luxury that could be taken or left. TV was getting to be a necessity.

Professional Sports as a Part Time Job

To give all this a little more perspective, the legendary Johnny Unitas was said to have played semi-pro football for $6.00 a game in 1955, one year before signing with the Baltimore Colts. In 1958 the starting center for Unitas' Colts was a guy named Buzz Nutter who earned a salary of $6,500 for the season which culminated in the Colts beating the Packers in a game some still contend was the greatest football game ever played. As late as 1968 the NFL's minimum salary was $10,000 per season. In 2006 however the average NFL salary had skyrocketed to $1.4 million per season.

So, in the late 50's and early 60's professional sports were often considered less than a serious full time career, generally unworthy of the kind of focus they get today. In fact it wasn't unusual to see top college athletes (i.e. Roger

Staubach) take a pass on the NFL, the NBA, or MLB in favor of a real job on which a family could be raised and supported. Nor was it unusual to see professional athletes selling insurance, real estate, or cars in the off season in order to make ends meet. In the late 50's and early 60's nobody became an instant millionaire through professional sports.

Sam's Personal Tug of War

In the case of Sam Coppola, athlete supreme from Stamford, CT, who had a family, a business, and numerous legitimate responsibilities and obligations, the incentives to throw all his eggs into one NFL basket were at best…questionable. The natural athlete side of Sam of course answered, "Yes, yes, a thousand times yes! I'm in!" But the husband, father, brother, son, and businessman side of him said, "Are you nuts? Why in the world would you roll the dice and take a chance on something like that? You could get seriously injured. What happens then?"

Wing Tips by Day, Cleats by Night

So, during the day, Sam Coppola chose to become a highly respected member of the Stamford, CT business community who concerned himself with generating jobs for Stamford Tile, Inc., hiring new staff, making payroll, balancing the books, and making monthly profit margins. He dabbled in real estate, discovering that serious money could be made from buying and selling land, single family homes, and commercial properties. With these activities Sam easily paid the mortgage, and put bread on the table for his family.

But after the ten hour work day (Sam was up every morning at 5:30 sharp) he left the business attire and acumen behind in favor of an alternative life on the football field (or the baseball diamond in the summer months) – practicing, playing, planning, strategizing, throwing, catching, kicking, blocking, running, hitting, fielding, scoring, and winning football and baseball games.

"The roar of the crowd coming to its feet in the wake of a well conceived, scoring play always sent shivers up and down my spine," Sam said. "I never got tired of the sounds, the thrills, the feel of the ball with my fingers gripping the laces just right, reading defenses, leading receivers just enough for them to catch the ball in full stride. The whole thing bordered on a religious experience for me. When I was on the field playing football, I felt like I was in the process of being who I was naturally meant to be. I was complete in a way that was unique in my life," he added.

The Stamford Tilers with Sam in the upper left and Mike upper right

The Golden Bears Had a Following

Despite the fact that all the networks had concentrated their bets on the NFL, the ACFC (Atlantic Coast Football Conference) still featured great athletes who attracted an enthusiastic, local following. "It wasn't unusual to see 3000 or 3500 people in the stands at kick off under the lights at Stamford High's football field on a Saturday evening in September or October," Sam said.

The local radio stations always broadcasted the games whether the Golden Bears were at home or away. If they were unable to attend, people would tune in and listen. On the following day the Stamford Advocate (the local newspaper) inevitably covered the game in detail, including photos.

"In those days people could attend a high school game on Friday night, a college game on Saturday afternoon, an ACFL game on Saturday evening, and they could watch the NFL on Sunday afternoon. We had our own niche that played an important role in the local sporting landscape," said Sam.

Ten Seasons in the ACFC

Sam spent ten seasons playing quarterback in the ACFC whose teams included the Stamford Golden Bears, as well as the Bridgeport (CT) Giants, the Flushing (NY) Vets, Port Chester (NY) Alfonso. Six of those seasons were spent playing with the Stamford Golden Bears, where Coach Al Shanen called all the plays, and Bruno Amato kept linebackers, defensive ends and tackles from sacking the quarterback. The next two seasons he spent with the Westchester Crusaders, and the last two were with the Milford Rockets. Sam called all the plays during his last four seasons. And during his decade in the ACFC he never played on a team with a losing record.

MVP and Good Knees

During that time Sam served as team captain or co-captain every year. He played in 8 championship games and won 6 of them. He led the league in passing 8 out ten seasons, and was named MVP 7 times. "In my very first season, Coach Shanen had a special brace made for my knee, and because of that brace and Bruno Amato, I never had a problem with the knee that I'd injured while playing in the Marines," Sam said.

The ACFC in 1958: the Flushing Vets

In 1958, Sam's second season, the Golden Bears came out of the gate with a perfect 6 and 0 record, as did their cross state rivals, the Flushing Vets. The Vets had actually not lost a game in over three years and came into the seventh game (against the Golden Bears) with a 35 game winning streak on the line and were two touchdown favorites.

> **The NFL in 1958**
>
> *In late December of 1958 Johnny Unitas and the Baltimore Colts defeated the New York Giants under blizzard conditions 23 to 17 in the first overtime ever played in an NFL Championship game. This game has since been dubbed by some as the greatest NFL game ever played. TV audiences were mesmerized by the event. It was this game that inspired Lamar Hunt to create the American Football League in order to compete with the NFL for a share of the professional football market.*

"We went into the Flushing Vets game a two touchdown underdog," said Sam, "and on the second play from scrimmage I completed a short pass to Allen Webb who proceeded to sprint the remaining 60 yards into the Vet's end zone. We scored in each of the first three quarters had 'em on their heels the entire game, which we won 19 to 13."

Dynamic Golden Bears Upset Flushing 19-
Coppola's Accurate Aerials
End Vets' 35-Game Streak
19-13

A Try Out With the New York Giants

Midway through the 1958 season Sam got a call asking if he'd like to attend a tryout for the New York Giants that was going to be held at Fordham's football field. He was informed there would be 40 players on hand, including three other quarterbacks. He decided to give it a shot.

"Charlie Conerly was the quarterback of the Giants that season, and when I arrived I shook hands with a couple of the scouts. I took a number of snaps from center and threw some passes to the receivers who had shown up for the same event. The scouts indicated they knew of my stats, "Sam said, "But I got the distinct feeling that they were looking for players who were a little younger than 28 years old. I mean Charlie Conerly was no spring chicken by then and I heard nothing back from the Giants after that."

The NFL in 1959

In 1959 oil magnet, gazillionaire Lamar Hunt of Dallas announced his intention to start a new professional football league to compete with the NFL. The name of the new league was The American Football League – the AFL

The ACFC in 1959: Richie Connors

During the 1959 season Sam met a guy named Richie Connors who he'd never forget. "Richie was playing linebacker for the Bridgeport Giants and I was having a good day against him. Every time I completed a pass he gave me this dirty look as if to say I'm going to kill you next time you do that. Fortunately Bruno kept Richie away from me the entire game and we won by a couple touchdowns."

"After the game Richie came up to shake hands. We both appreciated each other's talents. But he went further. He said that he'd like to play with the Golden Bears, and he wanted me to know that he'd spent time in prison for a drug problem. He swore though that he'd been clean for several years. I said he'd be welcome in the Golden Bears' camp and that he should contact Coach Al Shanen to make the appropriate arrangements. "

"Richie did as I suggested and played with the Golden Bears for the next two seasons. But I tell the Richie Connors story for another reason. This guy stood out to me because of his blunt honesty. He told me immediately about the drugs and the prison time. He didn't hide anything. Richie just said exactly what was on his mind. Looking back on my own football career, I now envy Richie's habit of speaking up and saying what was on his mind. If I'd been a little more like Richie in this regard, I may have made it in the NFL."

Sports Illustrated Spotlights Richie

Interestingly enough, a decade after Richie Connors played with Sam and the Golden Bears the entire sordid, yet colorful story of Richie's life was written up in a seven page article in Sports Illustrated (January 24, 1972) entitled, "What Made Richie Run? I still have a copy of that great article in a scrapbook somewhere in my office," Sam said.

The NFL in 1961

NBC was awarded a two-year contract for radio and television rights to the NFL Championship Game for $615,000 annually, $300,000 of which was to go directly into the NFL Player Benefit Plan, April 5, 1961.

Sam's Best Season, 1961

In his best season, 1961, Sam threw twenty six touchdowns in only nine games, one touchdown short of an average of three touchdown passes per game. As the result of this performance Sam was named 1961 league MVP.

September of 1961 was a busy time for Sam who was finishing off the baseball season with the Stamford Tilers and starting the football season with the Golden Bears.

"John Kelly and I were both playing on the same baseball team and the same football team," Sam said. "On two separate afternoons John and I played nine innings of baseball, and the minute that game was over we immediately drove to another field, equipment in hand, in order to play football. Our wives brought us both a change of clothes. We did a quick *Clark Kent* in the locker room, and proceeded to play four full quarters of football with the Golden Bears. Thinking back on it, I don't know when we slept."

Pistol Pete Saunders

At the beginning of the 1961 season a player named Pete Saunders tried to make the team as a wide receiver. "We called him Pistol Pete," Sam said, "and he was really a great athlete with speed, quickness, and moves that often left opposing players picking up their jock straps. But Pete lacked good hands. He'd get open almost every time he ran a pattern, I'd hit him with a pass, and he'd drop it time after time. Finally Coach Shanen dropped him from the squad one week before the first game of the season."

Pete Needed a Quarterback

But unbeknownst to Sam and his fellow Golden Bears, Pistol Pete left and joined a black league that had been organized down on the Jersey Shore. One evening Sam got a call from Pete who explained that his new team had a big game coming up, had lost their quarterback, and he wanted Sam to come and quarterback his team for one game.

"The game was on a bye week, there were no scheduling conflicts, so I told Pete that I'd be glad to help him out," Sam said. "I gathered up Bruno Amato, my main pass blocker, George Deenihan, my center, and Luke Malloy, my best receiver and we met Pete at the field."

"We were the only white folks in the stadium. We all played the entire game. And we won the game for Pistol Pete by two touchdowns, one of which was a twenty yard pass from me to Pistol Pete himself. If Coach Shanen had found out about that he'd have killed all four of us," Sam added.

The Portland Seahawks

During that same '61 season the Golden Bears traveled to Portland Maine to play the Portland Seahawks whose quarterback was a guy named Butch Songin. Songin had been the first quarterback for the New York Jets (when they played at Randall Island while Shea Stadium was being completed) before Broadway Joe came along. In that game Sam completed 26 of 28 passes and beat the home team by two touchdowns. "That was a game to remember," Sam said.

The NFL in 1962

The NFL entered into a single-network agreement with CBS for telecasting all regular-season games for $4.65 million annually, January 10, 1962.

Buying and Shuttering the Golden Bears

In the spring of 1962 Al Shanen approached Sam with the idea of the two of them buying the Golden Bears. At this point Shanen was coaching the local high school football team. But he said that if Sam would serve as player-coach, he thought it might work. Sam agreed, and he served as player-coach for the entire '62 season. But at the end of the year, with dwindling crowds, they decided it was time for the Golden Bears to close their doors.

Sam planned to retire from football in the wake of the Bears' demise. But in the summer of '63 he was approached by the Westchester Crusaders who wanted him to take over their quarterbacking duties. Sam agreed to take the job, but only if he could call all of his own plays. They agreed, and Sam spent two more productive seasons in the ACFC.

Finishing Off a Decade in the ACFC

Then in the spring of 1965 the Milford Rockets approached Sam and asked if he'd be willing to switch allegiances one more time. They also offered $300 dollars a game which in those days was good extra money. Sam agreed to another two year contract and he was allowed to call his own plays. At the end of the 1966 season however, and a full decade of quarterbacking, Sam decided it was finally time to hang his cleats up once and for all.

TV Corners the Pro Football Market

By the time the sun set on the 1966 season a decade after Sam Coppola had started his semi-pro football career, the odds of finding a TV set in the American home had grown exponentially, along with almost everything that the networks touched including the NBA, MLB, and more than any of the rest, the NFL. The stage was set for even bigger things to come when the NFL and the fledgling AFL merged in 1966.

A decade after Unitas and the Colts beat the Giants in "the greatest game ever played," Joe Namath captured the nation's attention in 1969 by upsetting the world champion Colts in Superbowl III. From that point forward the NFL grew like Jack's proverbial bean stalk, drawing more and more local attention away from semi pro leagues like the ACFC.

The NFL's decade of growth: 1957 to 1966*

1946-1955 – The Cleveland Browns along with Coach Paul Brown and quarterback Otto Graham dominated the NFL by appearing in 10 consecutive championship games, and winning 7 of them.

1957 - An NFL-record crowd of 102,368 saw the 49ers-Rams game at the Los Angeles Memorial Coliseum, November 10.

1958 - Baltimore, coached by Weeb Ewbank, defeated the Giants 23-17 in the first sudden-death overtime in an NFL Championship Game, December 28. The game ended when Colts fullback Alan Ameche scored on a one-yard touchdown run after 8:15 of overtime.

1959 - Lamar Hunt of Dallas announced his intentions to form a second pro football league. The new league was named the American Football League, August 22.

1960 - Pete Rozelle was elected NFL Commissioner as a compromise choice on the twenty-third ballot, January 26. Rozelle moved the league offices to New York City.

1961 - NBC was awarded a two-year contract for radio and television rights to the NFL Championship Game for $615,000 annually, $300,000 of which was to go directly into the NFL Player Benefit Plan, April 5.

1962 - The NFL entered into a single-network agreement with CBS for telecasting all regular-season games for $4.65 million annually, January 10.

1963 - The U.S. Fourth Circuit Court of Appeals reaffirmed the lower court's finding for the NFL in the $10-million suit brought by the AFL, ending three and a half years of litigation, November 21.

Jim Brown of Cleveland rushed for an NFL single-season record 1,863 yards.

1964 - The AFL signed a five-year, $36-million television contract with NBC to begin with the 1965 season, January 29.

CBS submitted the winning bid of $14.1 million per year for NFL regular-season television rights for 1964 & 1965, January 24.

CBS acquired the rights to the champion-ship games for 1964 and 1965 for $1.8 million per game, April 17.

Joe Namath signed a record three year contract for $427,000 with the New York Jets.

1965 - According to a Harris survey, sports fans chose professional football (41 percent) as their favorite sport, overtaking baseball (38 percent) for the first time, October.

Green Bay defeated Baltimore 13-10 in sudden-death overtime in a Western Conference playoff game. Don Chandler kicked a 25-yard field goal for the Packers after 13 minutes, 39 seconds of overtime, December 26. The Packers then defeated the Browns 23-12 in the NFL Championship Game, January 2.

1966 - The AFL-NFL war reached its peak, as the leagues spent a combined $7 million to sign their 1966 draft choices. The NFL signed 75 percent of its 232 draftees, the AFL 46 percent of its 181. Of the 111 common draft choices, 79 signed with the NFL, 28 with the AFL, and 4 went unsigned.

Pete Rozelle announced the NFL/AFL merger, June 8. Under the agreement, the two leagues would combine to form an expanded league with 24 teams, to be increased to 26 in 1968 and to 28 by 1970 or soon thereafter.

Congress approved the AFL-NFL merger, passing legislation exempting the agreement itself from antitrust action, October 21.

The rights to the Super Bowl for four years were sold to CBS and NBC for $9.5 million, December 13.

1969 - An AFL team won the Super Bowl for the first time, as the Jets defeated the Colts 16-7 at Miami, January 12 in Super Bowl III. The title Super Bowl was recognized by the NFL for the first time.

* The information on the preceding three pages, as well as the information in the side bars throughout the book, courtesy of the website http://www.nfl.com/history/chronology.

4

Winds Beneath the Wings

"Lots of people want to ride with you in the limo. But what you want is someone who will take the bus with you when the limo breaks down." **Oprah Winfrey**

Of Finnish descent, Millie House was born on November 16 of 1940, the third of four sisters. She grew up on a farm located about fifteen miles northeast of Rumford, Maine. Her father kept chickens, goats, pigs, and cows, and like most farm kids Millie became an early riser. When she was old enough and capable enough, she also began helping her parents with the multitude of chores.

"My dad normally kept about a hundred head of cattle on the farm," Millie said. "My three sisters and I helped him feed and water the animals, clean out stalls, and milk the cows. And this was a seven day a week job because the animals don't distinguish between weekends and weekdays."

In other words, when Millie House graduated from high school and accepted a telephone receptionist position in Stamford, CT, long, responsibility filled, Coppola-style days were already built into her DNA

Millie and Sam Meet

Millie and Sam met in the summer of 1961 when she moved from the dormitory where the telephone company's employees were housed, into an apartment complex that Sam happened to own. "When I met Sam he was my landlord and he initially struck me as a gentleman and a nice guy. When we started going out he told me that he was playing a baseball game that evening and he asked if I'd like to go and watch."

"I knew almost nothing about sports but I accepted Sam's invitation and I quickly found out that he was the team's star. Whether he was pitching or hitting he seemed to be the guy who was making things happen. As the baseball season faded and football season came to life Sam was now the quarterback and the center of attention for the Stamford Golden Bears. It felt like I was going out with a local celebrity," Millie said.

Mike Sr. Passes Away

Several months after Sam and Millie began going out Sam's father had a massive heart attack and died. "Sam had been so close with his dad for so long," Millie said. "Mike Sr's death mentally threw him for a loop, but we dug through it together. When the question came up about whether Sam should play football the next weekend, Eva (Sam's mom) and I both encouraged him to play. His dad would have wanted it that way. To this day I believe that football helped Sam get through that traumatic time in his life. All the turmoil also brought us closer together," she added.

As their relationship grew increasingly serious, they finally decided to get married in 1963. True to her upbringing, Millie began keeping the books for the various business enterprises that by now Sam was involved in. She was also taking an active role in the sporting side of the ledger as well.

Of Footballs and Tire Swings

"Every once in a while, Sam and I would take his dad's truck out to a local park," said Millie. "In the back end there were half-dozen footballs, an old truck tire, and a rope. We'd find a tree where Sam could hang the tire and he'd proceed to throw footballs through it from various distances, angles, standing still, or on the run, for an hour while I fielded 'em and threw 'em back."

"I was always amazed at how accurate Sam was with a football. I also knew the NFL was in the back of his mind and I wanted to help him get there if I could," Millie said. "In the meantime I clipped lots of newspaper articles and put them in a box until we had time to make a scrapbook."

However, with Stamford Tile depending on Sam, and with Millie managing the apartment complex which by now was generating a good income, and several real estate deals starting to pay off, the NFL remained a mirage sitting out there on the horizon, unconsummated, and just out of reach despite all the statistics Sam was piling up in the Atlantic Coast Football League.

The Quarterback Silently Hangs Up the Cleats

In late 1964 Millie became pregnant with their first child and on August 16 of 1965 Sam Jr. was born. With this new development Millie was forced to slow down in order to be the mother that she wanted to be. And by the time the sun went down on the 1966 season, Sam had turned 36 and he decided it was time to hang up his cleats.

"He was still physically capable of playing football," Millie said. "But he just had too many things on his plate and he knew it. Despite having Mary McCourt (babysitter supreme) helping out with the kids, if Sam was going to be a good father to Sammy Jr., he was going to have to give up something and football really was the only viable candidate."

The NFL in 1994
*A 1994 study of 7,000 former players by the **National Institute of Occupational Safety and Health** found linemen had a 52 percent greater risk of dying from heart disease than the general population. While U.S. life expectancy is 77.6 years, recent studies suggest **the average for NFL players is 55, 52 for linemen**. The average career length is a little over 3 years.*

Sam's Reputation Leads the Way

As much as he resisted retirement, Sam's athletic reputation continued into the future and it played a role in his business success. "For ten years the Stamford Tilers were always at the top of their division and Sam was always pitching a one hitter (one season he won the pitching crown), knocking in the winning run, leading the league in hitting (one season he actually hit 419), or making a miraculous one handed grab at third base," Millie said.

"For those ten years the Atlantic Coast Football Conference was Sam's playground in the fall," she said. "It seemed like his name was always in the Stamford Advocate headlines. Without ever being aware of it, Sam was his own walking, talking, running, and throwing public relations agency generating great press in such a way that everyone in town knew of him, and on occasion that reputation helped open the doors to new business opportunities."

Sam's Best Friend Tom Uva

Throughout the 50's and 60's Sam's closest friend was a former high school classmate named Tom Uva. Tom was never an athlete, but he was a bit of an adventurer as was Sam and they got along real well. By the time Sam had returned from the service and had married Millie, Tom had developed a TV repair business with which he supported his wife and children nicely.

"Oddly enough Sam's birthday was July 23rd and Tom's was July 24th," Millie said. "On a number of occasions we went out to a birthday dinner with Tom and Ceil. We'd celebrate Sam's birthday, and then at the stroke of midnight we'd switch to celebrating Tom's birthday."

In the summer of 1966 Millie became pregnant with child number two. A couple of days later Sam called Tom to announce the news, and before the conversation was over Sam told Tommy that if the new child was a boy he was going to name him after his best friend. "Tommy was flattered beyond belief," Millie said. "Then on March 26th 1967, I delivered a healthy baby boy who immediately, on the spot was named Tom."

Tragedy Strikes Again

During that same time period Tom Uva decided that he wanted to learn to fly so he talked Sam into taking some flying lessons with him. The wackiness of Sam's schedule caused him to stop after a couple lessons, but Tom continued for several months until he finally got his pilot's license. "Tommy was real proud of getting that license," Millie said.

One Saturday afternoon in the fall of 1969 Tom called Sam and told him that he and two mutual friends Frank Faugno and Phil Pertuccio, along with Phil's step-son Mike who'd survived being shot up in Viet Nam, were flying to Boston the next day to have Mike checked out. Tom asked if Sam would like to come along, but Sam had already scheduled a trip to the Italian Center Festival on Sunday with Tommy and Sammy Jr., so he had to decline Tom's offer.

Phil, JoJo, and Tom (L to R) at a banquet

"Tom, Phil, and Mike took off from Greenwich (CT) airport at about 11 PM on Sunday evening," Millie said. "And according to the reports, they ran into trouble immediately. They tried to set the plane down on a local golf course fairway, but on the way down it became entangled with a tree and exploded, killing all four passengers instantly."

Once again Sam was devastated. First it was his dad in 1961, and now his best friend in 1969. Tom was only 37 years old when he died leaving his wife Ceil, three children, and one on the way, with no husband and no father.

"We attended the funeral and all the caskets were closed because of the damage the explosion had done to their bodies. Sam and I will never forget the good times we had with Tom and Ceil," said Millie.

The NFL in 1969
An AFL team (the New York Jets with QB Joe Willie Namath) won the Super Bowl for the first time, as the Jets defeated the heavily favored Baltimore Colts 16-7 at Miami, January 12 in Super Bowl III. The title Super Bowl was recognized by the NFL for the first time.

The Roaring '70's

The late 60's and early 70's were a very busy time for Sam, Millie, and their new family. Stamford Tile was growing by leaps and bounds under Sam and Mike Jr. The House of Tile was going gangbusters thanks to Millie and Laurel.

"Next door to the House of Tile was a building that Sam became interested in and he decided to check it out," Millie said. "Sam went to the courthouse, talked to a couple of real estate people and he decided he could get a good deal on this piece of property. So he bought it and started a real estate company called Coppola Properties. He hired a guy named Bob Annuzzi who was good at supervising the jobs, and another guy named Charlie Saverine, an engineering type who did all the architectural drawings for Coppola Properties.

We really could have used another twenty four hours in each day," she added.

Charlie and Rita Magyar

Once a year, however, Sam and Millie took one week out of their ultra busy schedule in order to go somewhere on vacation. In June of 1972 they boarded a jet on their way to Puerto Rico where they planned to spend a week basking in sunshine on a sandy beach alongside the Atlantic Ocean.

As they took their seats Sam heard a friendly voice say "Sam Coppola." He looked down and he saw a gentleman named Charlie Magyar for whom Sam had done some tiling work several months before. Charlie's hand was outstretched towards Sam, who responded with his own hand for the shaking and thus began a conversation that has lasted now for the better part of four decades.

"We spent a high percentage of that week in Puerto Rico with Charlie and his wife Rita," Millie said, "and we got to know each other well enough that our relationship continued once we arrived back home. We did all kinds of things together from dinners, to dancing, and attending the casino. Sam and Charlie became lifelong friends."

The NFL 1973

The Buffalo Bills moved their home games from War Memorial Stadium to Rich Stadium in nearby Orchard Park. The Giants tied the Eagles 23-23 in the final game in Yankee Stadium, September 23. The Giants played the rest of their home games at the Yale Bowl in New Haven, Connecticut.

*A rival league, **the World Football League**, was formed and was reported in operation, October 2. It had plans to start play in 1974.*

*O.J. Simpson of Buffalo became the first player to rush for **more than 2,000 yards in a season**, gaining 2,003.*

Paces, the Night Club

In 1973 Charlie opened a night club that he called "Paces," which was Rita's maiden name. After several months he and Sam were talking about the club and Charlie said that he wasn't making the kind of money that he was expecting to make when he opened the place up. Sam asked if Charlie was using a counter at the door so he'd know how many customers were attending each evening. Much to Sam's surprise Charlie said he was not using a counter.

"With that thought in mind Charlie asked Sam if he'd do the collecting for a couple evenings in order to see what the difference might be?" said Millie. "Sam told Charlie that his tight schedule wouldn't allow it. Charlie responded by saying that he knew Sam had Saturday nights free and so they agreed that on the following Saturday night, Sam would do all the collecting at the door."

When the evening was over and the counting had finished Charlie informed Sam that he'd collected three times the revenue that had been collected on any previous Saturday night. Charlie was being ripped off. This locked Sam into a Saturday night job for one solid year after which Sam had to resign over the time required by his own enterprises.

Puerto Rico II

Later that same year ('74) Charlie took Sam on an all expenses paid trip (Sam insisted on picking up all the tips) to Puerto Rico. They packed their golf clubs because Charlie was an avid golfer. When they arrived in San Juan Charlie's clubs were on the baggage turntable, but Sam's failed to show up.

Charlie kidded that Sam's clubs had been lost in transit. But after 45 minutes of waiting, they finally reported the lost clubs to the carrier's office in the airport.

In the wake, Sam rented clubs and a pair of golf shoes that resulted in 18 holes of foot misery. Despite the golf faux pas, Sam and Charlie spent a week in Puerto Rico that was loaded with sunshine, great food, and superb company.

Once back in New York, Charlie asked if Sam would drop him off at home (he was exhausted) and close down Paces. Sam consented. Ironically, Sam's golf clubs showed up once he and Charlie arrived back in New York.

Petrina and Charlie

On the home front, Millie became pregnant for the third time and Charlie Magyar made it a point of saying he wanted to be the first to see the new baby after the parents. On July 5th, 1975 a 7 lb, 13 oz baby girl named Petrina Coppola was born, and much to Sam and Millie's surprise Charlie and Rita showed up in the hospital and were indeed the first to see her after Sam, Millie, and the two boys.

"To this day Charlie and Petrina stay in touch and have a very special relationship which stems directly from Charlie's original interest in her," said Millie. "Charlie and Rita are also still very close friends of ours. In fact it was Charlie who insisted that someone should wrap a book around Sam's astounding story, and now here we are in the process of doing exactly that. Thanks Charlie," Millie added.

Big Mike, Bruno the Bodyguard and Coach Shanen

"We don't stop playing because we get old. We get old because we stop playing." **George Bernard Shaw**

Michael Jr. was the youngest of the Coppola brothers, born on June 29, 1932, a full two years after Sam. And with a full two years between Sam and Mike there never was much in the way of a sibling rivalry that often interferes with the relationships of brothers who are closer in age.

"Sam was not only a great natural athlete in his own right," said Mike, "but he was a big brother in every sense. In other words, I always looked up to Sam and he always looked out after me in the west side Italian neighborhood where we grew up. Everybody should be lucky enough to have a big brother who's willing and able to lead the way, and introduce them to the world. That's what Sam always did in my case."

The brothers, who always looked out after each other, spent countless summer days that began with Ma Coppola packing sack lunches for Sammy and Mike before they grabbed the mitts, bats, and balls and hiked a mile and a half to Woodside Park in order to play baseball against teams from other neighborhoods who showed up on a regular basis looking for a challenge.

The Organizer in Chief

"On our side Sam was always the organizer who got the word out to kids up and down Spruce Street," said Mike. "He'd communicate with kids from the other teams to set up times (usually in the morning) when we were going to meet."

Sam was inevitably his team's best pitcher. When he wasn't on the mound Sam was fielding line drives and red hot grounders at third base. And regardless of what position Sam was playing, he was always knocking the baseball all over the ball park. "I guess you could say that my big brother Sam was my first sports hero," Mike said. "And I was always proud that he was my brother and to be on his team."

In the fall, after school, the game became three on three football until supper time. Sam quarterbacked while Mike ran the ball, caught the ball, and blocked for Sam.

"We'd come in for supper when my dad got home and we'd be sweaty and dirty so Ma would make us clean up before we sat down to eat. But as Sam and JoJo would both testify, Ma always made that evening meal worthy of sitting down to," Mike said. "We may not have been rolling in dough back then, but you'd never know it from Ma Coppola's home cooking. I guess she didn't want us to be skinny."

Football Under the Street Lights

Occasionally, when they convinced their parents that they didn't have much homework, Mike and Sam were allowed to go out after supper and play under the street lights. "We always thought that was so cool because that's where the high school kids played football – under the lights. And back then we didn't have all the gangs, drugs, and violence that kids have to contend with today," Mike added.

When he attended Cloonan Junior High, Sam won the city boxing championship for his age. Two years later Mike decided to give boxing a try as well. "I went out for boxing one season when I was attending Cloonan and I had fun learning how to handle myself in the ring. But at the end of the season I didn't have any medals to show for it like Sam did," Mike said. "After that I concentrated on baseball."

In 1947 Sam and Mike Jr. were both attending St. Basil High School and it was the only year in which the Coppola brothers found themselves playing together on the same school baseball team. "I played right field and as usual Sam was our team's best pitcher. And if he wasn't pitching he was playing third base because nobody ever wanted Sam sitting on the bench unless they were playing for the other team," Mike said. "And as I recall, we made it a point to never give the other team a vote in that decision."

Never Saw a Sport Sam Couldn't Play

"I don't know that I ever saw a sport that Sam was bad at. He was naturally strong, pretty fast, and he was extremely well coordinated," Mike said. And those qualities go a long way in any athletic event. Sam could have picked up a ping pong paddle and been a great ping pong player. He was a natural athlete. I don't know how else to say it."

Mike went into the service (the Army drafted him in 1951) a couple of years before Sam did and he spent a couple of years in Germany playing baseball for the base where he was stationed.

"I had great experiences in the service because my main responsibility was playing baseball. Near the end of my tour of duty the baseball season came to an end and in order to remain in the sporting arena I told my commanding officer that I could box. Other than the one year in Cloonan Junior High, that was the only other time I boxed." Mike said.

$5000 to Sign and $400 a Month

"When I was discharged in 1954 I tried out for, and signed a minor league baseball contract with the Kansas City A's, who had originally been the Philadelphia A's and who are now the Oakland Athletics," Mike said.

"My contract called for a signing bonus of $5,000 and a monthly salary of $400 dollars. And because of my ability to hit the long ball, I was always the best paid player on any team that I played for. So you can imagine what the other guys were being paid. But in reality, $400 a month wasn't all that bad back then. Today things are different," he added.

When Sam got out of the Marines and they met up in Virginia where Mike was playing with the Wytheville (VA) Athletics, he'd already decided that he was tired of the infinite bus trips up and down the east coast, even if he was playing baseball, the game he'd always loved.

"I decided that I could do better working for my dad at Stamford Tile," Mike said. "So when the season ended, I resigned, jumped into my pink T-Bird with Sam and drove home to Stamford. My dad was a little disappointed because he always loved sports so much. But after I explained the whole situation he gave my decision his blessing and put me to work. I spent the next 40 years working for Stamford Tile and House of Tile living in my home town, and to this day I never regretted quitting professional baseball. "

The Twilight League

Of course that didn't mean that Michael and Sam quit playing baseball. When they got home Mike Sr. decided to sponsor a team in the regional Twilight Baseball League. He called his new team the Stamford Tilers. Mike Jr. and Sam of course played 8 seasons with the Tilers.

"We used to play every Sunday morning. Sam was the league's dominant pitcher, and one year he even won the batting title with a 400 plus batting average, like Ted Williams," Mike said. "He never quite kept up with me though when it came to hitting home runs," he confessed.

Mike Attended All of Sam's Games

With the exception of the two years he spent in the service, Mike made it his business to attend every game that Sam played for Fordham. He also attended every game that Sam quarterbacked for the Golden Bears.

"Sam talked me into playing one year with the Golden Bears," said Mike. "I played offensive guard and linebacker. But I'd finish a game with a pile of bruises while Sam was being protected by the likes of Bruno Amato and Al Shanen's (The Golden Bear's coach) special knee brace. He'd finish the game with a relatively clean uniform."

"One year was all the semi-pro football I needed. From that point on I became a football spectator who sat in the stands rooting for my big brother to throw touchdown passes. Baseball was my sport and I should have avoided the Golden Bears. Hind sight is always 20/20" he added.

> **The NFL in 1964**
> *CBS submitted the winning bid of $14.1 million per year for the NFL regular-season television rights for 1964 and 1965. CBS acquired the rights to the championship games for 1964 and 1965 for $1.8 million per game. On April 17th, Pete Gogolak of Cornell signed a contract with Buffalo, becoming the first soccer-style kicker in pro football.*

And Most Amazing...

And the most amazing thing, according to Mike, was that all this was going on while Sam was putting in ten hour days at Stamford Tile, making real estate deals on the side, being a good husband and father, while taking care of JoJo and Ma after Mike Sr. had passed away.

"Everyone in the Coppola family was a hard worker," Mike said. "Our parents were our role models in that regard. They built that characteristic into our DNA. But Sam was different. He was a human tornado."

"He was up early, took care of a million different business details every day, all week long. But then he'd find time to be a good husband to Millie and father to his own kids, while dropping in on Ma and JoJo on a regular basis. Then he played football and baseball in his spare time. I often wondered when he slept or if he slept. His energy level was higher that anyone I've ever known. When I look back on all that, it's really kind of amazing," he added.

Bruno the Body Guard

Golden Bears Fullback Bruno Amato however, always contended that Sam Coppola was not very good when he was laying flat on his back. Sam always agreed with Bruno on this, and most other issues, wholeheartedly.

In that light it was Bruno's primary responsibility to make sure that Sam was allowed to remain upright and vertical, and that he had enough time to locate his receivers downfield, and complete his passes.

"As long as he was protected," Bruno said, "Sam Coppola was lethal throwing the football. Like Brett Favre or Kurt Warner today, if we gave Sam time to throw, he'd cut the other team to ribbons with his passing.

"Now that I look back on it, it's really too bad that the Giants, the Jets, or the Eagles missed out on Sam. With the right opportunity he'd have been up there with Van Brocklin, Tittle, or Graham. Who knows? Sam was a great quarterback as long as he had time to throw the ball," Bruno said.

Built From the Ground Up

As far as Bruno himself was concerned, the 5' 9", 200 pound Stamford native was built like a fire hydrant from the ground up. You see, starting at the youthful age of 12 Bruno was expected to work in his family's business, which was manufacturing headstones for local cemeteries.

"Some of these stones could weigh 1500 to 1800 pounds apiece and I was expected to move these monsters from one place to another using only a hand truck. As the result of this experience I developed really strong legs and hips which enabled me to be very quick on the football field. I couldn't run very far, but for 20 yards I'd beat everyone on the team, including Sam," said Bruno

Bruno and Sam

In any case, it was those piston-like legs that allowed Bruno to continually torpedo oncoming blockers in the process of giving Sam enough time to complete a high percentage of his passes. "Sam really had only one weakness, and that was the fact that he was so busy filling the air with passes that he neglected to hand the ball off to me enough times – just kidding," Bruno said.

The game that stands out in Bruno's mind is The Golden Bear's upset victory over the Flushing Vets. "These guys hadn't lost a game in years, and they were heavy favorites to kick our butts. Coach Shanen called all the plays, and Sam threw a pass to Allen Webb that went for a 66 yard touchdown on the second play of the game. He was in some kind of a zone the entire afternoon. I don't know if he missed a pass all day," said Bruno. "It was as close to perfect as I ever remember a quarterback being. It was like the Jets upsetting the Colts in 1969. I'll remember the Flushing Vets game as long as I live."

The NFL in 1966

A series of secret meetings regarding a possible AFL-NFL merger were held in the spring of 1966 between Lamar Hunt of Kansas City and Tex Schramm of Dallas. Rozelle announced the merger, June 8. Under the agreement, the two leagues would combine to form an expanded league with 24 teams

Coach Shanen

In the late '50's and early '60's sophistication had yet to become a part of football's culture. As a matter of fact, according the Coach Al Shanen, the Stamford Golden Bears lacked all kinds of accoutrements that a modern Pop Warner League team would take for granted today.

For example, they lacked a grass field on which to practice, so they worked out on St. Cecelia's blacktop parking lot in sneakers instead of cleats. This meant that all scrimmage and all practice contact were eliminated. They had no blocking sleds, no tackling dummies, no training rooms, and no statisticians. This also meant they didn't keep statistics other than won and loss percentages.

Drawing on the Grass

In Shanen's words, "When I was coaching the Golden Bears I didn't even have a clip board on which to draw up plays. Instead I'd pull Sam over on the sidelines, draw a play out in the grass, and he was so good that he could go back into the huddle, call the play, and make it work. Sam was loaded with talent, but one of his greatest talents was his ability to quickly and successfully adapt to new situations. Whatever I asked Sam to do, he'd find a way to pull it off," Shanen said. "That's just the kind of athlete he was."

Shanen tried to position the Golden Bears as the taxi squad to the Giants and the Titans (now the Jets) of the old American Football League. He spoke on several occasions to Giants General Manager Andy Robustelli but the owner, Wellington Mara was not interested in taking on any more liability than he already had, so a formal affiliation was never consummated with either the Giants or the Titans.

> **The NFL from 1945 to 1955**
> *When the Cleveland Browns dominated the NFL, Coach Paul Brown's team included a dozen players over and above his official 32 man roster. He'd get these guys jobs driving taxi cabs in Cleveland. They'd work out with the team, and if an injury occurred and he needed a replacement he immediately went to what he called his "**taxi squad**."*

The relationship was close enough however that there was one Golden Bears game that Shanen coached on a Friday evening, and two days later, two of his players, Allen Webb, and Johnny Counts were in the New York Giants starting backfield on Sunday afternoon. That's the level of talent that permeated the ACFC in those days.

Race in Baltimore

There was a second occasion when Shanen had scheduled the Bears to play an exhibition game in Baltimore. They took a Greyhound Bus (regarded as a symbol of Civil Rights back then) to Baltimore, played the game, and when they were done, Coach Shanen asked the opposing coach to recommend a good place for the Bears to eat. The opposing coach looked at Shanen like he was crazy and proceeded to let him know that nobody in Baltimore would serve his team because he had Negro players on it.

"At that point one of the opposing team's black players signaled to Allen Webb, and said for us to follow him. We boarded the Greyhound and proceeded to follow this guy into the blackest neighborhood in Baltimore. He pulled up in front of a restaurant/bar and motioned for us to come inside. We did. We ate. We drank. And we had an unbelievably great time until 2:30 or 3 in the morning," Shanen said.

"When it came time to pay the bill I discovered that we didn't have enough money. The owner looked directly at me and said that we had been the first white folks who'd ever stepped foot inside his establishment. He was so happy that the bill was going to be on him. It was an experience that both Sam and I will never forget," Shanen said.

Sam Completed 80% of His Passes

According to Coach Shanen, Sam Coppola was a genetically gifted, natural athlete who combined his natural talents with the habit of hard work and intelligence...a hard combination to beat. "Sam was also an exciting guy to be around. He led an exciting life. He was overflowing with energy and his enthusiasm rubbed off on the other players. He was positively contagious," Shanen said.

Coppola's Aerial Completions Top ACL Percentages

NEW YORK — The Providence Steamrollers and Paterson Miners,, both undefeated in the Atlantic Coast Football League to date, will seek undisputed possession of first place Saturday night, when they meet at Paterson's Hinchcliffe Stadium. Frankfort plays at Ansonia in another circuit encounter, Saturday night.

"Sam also had an incredibly quick release, a great passion for the game of football, and although we didn't keep statistics back then, I know Sam completed at least 80% of his passes during his six years with the Golden Bears. He had all the tools to make it in the NFL, but for some reason the opportunity never came along," Shanen said. "Both he and Bruno Amato deserved to make it in the big time."

Three of the Best Football Players
I Ever Knew

"I had a friend was a big baseball player back in high school
He could throw that speedball by you
Make you look like a fool boy
Saw him the other night at this roadside bar,
I was walking in, he was walking out
We went back inside sat down had a few drinks
all he kept talking about was
Glory days well they'll pass you by
Glory days in the wink of a young girl's eye
Glory days, glory days, glory days"
Bruce Springsteen

Al Fenaroli grew up in the heart of New York City in the 30's and 40's, and when he was old enough he began pitching in with the family's moving business. "By the time I was out of high school I'd been in every neighborhood in the city pushing a hand truck full of lord knows what," said Fenaroli. "On a number of occasions I went head over heels, picked myself up off the ground, and kept on pushing the hand truck. That could be construed as good training for a future football player I'd suppose," he added.

Fenaroli attended Fordham Prep High School where at 6'2", 237 lbs, he was a starting offensive and defensive tackle for the football team. Al was also an excellent student and when he graduated he was awarded a full athletic scholarship to play football at Fordham.

Sam Coppola's Roommate

When he arrived on campus he was assigned a roommate from Stamford, CT named Sam Coppola who was listed as an offensive and defensive halfback. Fenaroli the tackle and Coppola the halfback became fast friends and remained roommates for their entire four years at Fordham.

One of the things that Sam shared in common with his Fordham teammate, Al Fenaroli, was the fact that Al had a sister who had the same kinds of challenges as JoJo. It's one of the intangibles that made these two football teammates, friends forever. "In those four years Sam and I never had a bad word between us," Fenaroli said, "which is kind of amazing when you sit back and think about it."

Back in the early 50's, freshmen were ineligible to play varsity ball, so both Fenaroli and Coppola both started every game for the freshman squad. "I was injured early in our sophomore year but Sam played a lot of ball that season," said Fenaroli. "But we both started throughout our junior and senior years, often playing both ways (offense and defense) which was not all that unusual in those days."

AL FENAROLI

Don't Kick the Ball to Ollie Matson

When they were juniors, Fordham played a game against the University of San Francisco who at that time had the great Ollie Matson as well as Gino Marchetti who was a perennial All Pro with the Baltimore Colts.

"I remember the coaches warning us before the game started to avoid kicking the ball to Ollie Matson. But on the opening kickoff our kicker made a mistake, Matson fielded the ball and took the ball back 90 some yards for a touchdown on the very first play of the game. "

"We got the ball back, drove down field, and tied the score. And once again the coach warned our kicker about Matson. Would you believe that he kicked the ball in exactly the same place and Matson repeated his 90 yard TD run all over again – instant replay. They were a touchdown ahead and their offense had yet to be on the field," Fenaroli said.

Don't Lose Your Cool

Late in the same game the score was tied. Suddenly a Fordham player got mad at a San Francisco player. With no face masks back then, he punched the guy in the nose. "We got penalized 15 yards, and they proceeded to march down field and score the final touchdown of the game," Fenaroli said. "We lost the San Francisco/Ollie Matson game by one touchdown because one of our guys lost his cool."

The NFL from 1946-1955
The Cleveland Browns along with Coach Paul Brown and hall of fame quarterback Otto Graham dominated the NFL by appearing in 10 consecutive NFL championship games, and winning 7 of them.

The Class Beer Party

But it wasn't all football and books. Every year their class would host a beer party at a local establishment where the owners would decorate the place in school colored crepe paper, among other things.

"One year Sam and I went down to one of these class beer parties and somebody poured beer on Sam's head," Fenaroli said. And somehow the crepe paper came down on top of him about the same time and Sam ended up with maroon and white hair."

"When we got back to the dorm we decided to wash the colors out of Sam's hair with the only thing we found to do it with - toothpaste. So that's what we used. The beer undoubtedly helped us make that decision."

The Occasional Game of Poker

Like many college students back then, Al and Sam and a few other guys would occasionally get together over a friendly game of poker. "For some reason I've always been a terrible poker player but Sam was good and he'd always win all the money. When the game was over and we'd go back to our room, Sam would always give all the money I'd lost back to me," Fenaroli said.

"But that's how Sam was. He was always quiet, low key, and yet very talented. We've been great friends ever since our days at Fordham," he added

Sam's Great Head of Hair

The one other story Al likes to tell on Sam was that he was always concerned about losing his hair. As the result he was always checking himself in the mirror to make sure it was still all intact.

"But when we got together about four years ago," Fenaroli said, "Sam was in his mid seventies and he still had a full head of hair, unlike me. I will admit however, that without all my guidance Sam would never have made it through college," he said with a chuckle. "Those were wonderful times for both Sam and I, and I'd wager that neither one of us will ever forget them."

After graduating from Fordham, Sam joined the Marines for two years where he played a lot more football and baseball. When he was discharged in '56 and returned to Stamford he found a new opportunity to express himself athletically. A former Stamford High quarterback named Dennis Behunick had started a new semi-pro football team that he called the Stamford Golden Bears.

Dennis Behunick

Dennis (Whitey) Behunick was discharged from the Marines in 1954. He moved back home to Stamford, got married, and one weekend he traveled with his new wife to Franklin, NJ to see a friend play semi-pro football for the Franklin Miners of the Atlantic Coast Football Conference.

"When I went down to see my buddy after the game he introduced me to the Miners coach who recruited me on the spot, and I ended up playing quarterback the last seven games of the season for them, before sustaining a rib injury in the second quarter of the last game," Behunick said.

The Golden Bears Kicked Off

"But the experience made me think that we should have a semi-pro team in Stamford. So I got together with a friend named Mike Potenza and started the team we called The Golden Bears in the fall of 1956."

Behunick's first recruit was a local football hero named Bruno Amato, who'd starred at Stamford High School, had been recruited by the University of Dayton and banged up his knee in early practice his freshman year. He returned home and helped out in the family business instead of playing college football. "Bruno was about 5' 10" tall, but he played like he was 230 or 240. He was one of the best football players I'd ever seen and I knew we could build a football team around Bruno, Behunick said."

In year one Behunick was not only playing quarterback, but he was also coaching and managing the Golden Bears, which meant he was operating on overload. In year two he backed out of playing, hired Al Shanen (himself an All American at University of Dayton) to coach the Bears, and recruited Sam Coppola to play quarterback.

Concentrated on Managing

"This allowed me to concentrate on managing the team. And with Al, Bruno, and Sam all on board, the Golden Bears really started to gel in '57," said Behunick.

The Bears had a friend in a local sports writer named "Moe" Magliola who dedicated lots of ink to the team, which in turn generated some enviable crowds. Behunick and Potenza recruited other local talent that represented potential NFL timber, and the interest continued to grow.

Andy Robustelli and the New York Giants

Behunick knew Andy Robustelli who was a Stamford native, and several times an All Pro defensive end for the New York Giants. By this time Robustelli was serving as the Giants General Manager, and Dennis asked him to co-sign a note on behalf of the Bears to get uniforms. Robustelli consented and the Bears got their uniforms, along with one more little present in the deal.

"Andy happened to have Paul Brown's offensive playbook in his office and he said that the Brown's offensive system was much simpler than the Giant's system. He also suggested that our guys could benefit from running it. I gladly accepted that information and we implemented the Brown's system which in the end had lots to do with the Golden Bear's success," Behunick said.

> **The NFL in 1962**
> *The Western Division defeated the Eastern Division 47-27 in the first AFL All-Star Game, played before 20,973 in San Diego, January 7. Both leagues prohibited grabbing any player's facemask. The AFL voted to make the scoreboard clock the official timer of the game. The NFL entered into a single-network agreement with CBS for telecasting all regular-season games for $4.65 million annually, January 10, 1962.*

Sam Forgot His Knee Brace

"I remember one game we were playing against the Bridgeport Giants when Sam had forgot to bring his knee brace. So I raced out of the stadium to get it," Behunick said.

"By the time I returned the second quarter had started and Sam had already thrown three touchdown passes. I looked at him and asked if he wasn't better off without the brace. Sam was a tough, hard nosed football player who often played through injuries. But the last thing the Golden Bears needed was for Sam to reinjure his knee. Needless to say he put the brace on and went back into the game."

Reading the Riot Act Produced Blocking

In another game against the Franklin Miners (Franklin, NJ) Sam was getting knocked around and beat up on every other play. For some reason Shanen was unable to make it to that game and Behunick had to take over the coaching reins.

"We went into the locker room at halftime and I read the riot act to our guys. I mean, I used every word that I'd ever learned in the Marines Corps, and when we went back out for the second half, Sam suddenly became untouchable. We were suddenly blocking, Sam was now completing almost all his passes, and despite the fact that they hadn't lost on their home field in five years, we ended up winning that game by a couple touchdowns," Behunick mused.

Dedicated, Passionate, and Tough

"All in all we had a great six year run and Sam Coppola was in the middle of that entire experience," Behunick said. "He was dedicated and passionate about the game of football. He was always putting in extra practice time with his receivers so that their timing was like clockwork. On top of that he was tough as nails and almost impossible to hurt. And when Bruno Amato was blocking for him, he was almost impossible to reach. With the right breaks, Sam, Bruno, and Toto DeLuca all had NFL written all over them."

Tony "Toto" Deluca

Standing 6'2" tall and weighing 255, Tony DeLuca was the 1955 captain of his high school football team in Greenwich, CT. Upon graduation he was recruited by Kansas University the same year as the (7' 1") late, great Wilt (the Big Dipper) Chamberlain arrived from his hometown of Philadelphia. "Actually Wilt and I had the same guidance counselor our freshman years," said DeLuca. "And Wilt was someone I always looked up to."

But when Tony returned home to Stamford after his freshman year he discovered that he was needed by the family's hauling and excavating business, so he decided against returning to Lawrence for his sophomore year. "DeLuca Excavating is now in its 50th year and my kids are the fourth generation overseeing it. I couldn't be more proud of each and every one of them, 'DeLuca said. "But it was the responsibilities that go along with a family owned business that caused me to take a pass on finishing up at K.U."

A year after returning from K.U., Tony was introduced to the Stamford Golden Bears. It was 1957, the same year that Sam Coppola came on board. That introduction began a six year stint as a defensive tackle under Coach Al Shanen. The only interruption came in 1960 when the world champion Green Bay Packers invited Tony to attend training camp.

The Green Bay Interruption

"I was in Green Bay for about a month," DeLuca said. "The great Vince Lombardi was the head coach, Bart Starr was the quarterback, Paul Hornung was the feature running back, and Jimmy Taylor from LSU was the fullback. Lombardi wanted me to play defensive end because of my speed. I had a good several weeks with the Packers and I thought I'd made the team. But at the last minute I got cut. When I look back on it I had a chance to sign with several other teams where my odds of making it would have been much better than with the reigning world champs. But hind sight is always 20/20 and I still have some great memories of that experience."

DeLuca remembers Lombardi as a no-nonsense, *my way or the highway* kind of coach. "I remember that every Wednesday was the player's night off and a bunch of them would always go out drinking. One Thursday morning, the day after a Wednesday night party, Emlen Tunnell, the former great New York Giants defensive back was on the field puking his guts out when Lombardi told him to hurry up or get the hell off the field. In Green Bay, the Lord and Vince Lombardi were on about the same level," DeLuca said.

Shanen the Gentleman's Gentleman

Lombardi was a stark contrast to the Golden Bears coach Al Shanen who was a gentleman's gentleman and a student of football. "In that sense Shanen was the opposite of Lombardi," said DeLuca. "On the Golden Bears everyone was working a day job and squeezing football in at night and on the weekends. We all just loved playing football. Shanen understood that and he made the game fun for everyone."

Coppola, DeLuca, Deenihan Vital To Westchester Crusaders' Bid

Having Sam Coppola at quarterback was one big reason why the Golden Bears always had winning seasons. And of course winning seasons are a lot more fun than losing seasons. "Sam was an amazing athlete who always put in the extra time required to make sure that he and his offensive unit were on the same page. The timing between Sam and LeRoy Vaughn, Luke Molloy, Don Goings, or Allen Webb was unbelievable. Given a little time Sam would rip any defense to shreds regardless of what level he was playing," DeLuca said.

Sports & Race Relations in the 50's and 60's

"No one is born hating another person because of the color of his skin, or his background, or his religion. People must be taught to hate, and if they can be taught to hate, they can learn to love, for love comes more naturally to the human heart than hatred. "
Nelson Mandela

In 1957 when Sam Coppola began quarterbacking for Coach Al Shanen and the Stamford Golden Bears, Jim Crow laws were still solidly intact throughout the American south. Martin Luther King had yet to launch the Civil Rights movement, the Voting Rights Act had yet to be signed into law by future President Lyndon Baines Johnson, while the Negro (baseball) League, and the Globetrotters (basketball) provided limited sporting opportunities for black athletes.

On the other hand, Jackie Robinson had broken the color barrier in Major League Baseball, Chuck Cooper and Sweetwater Clifton had done the same in the National Basketball Association. Bill Russell, K.C. Jones, and Sam Jones were playing basketball for Red Auerbach and the Boston Celtics, and the legendary Paul Brown had been ignoring the NFL Owner's ban on African American athletes for a decade and dominating professional football.

Italian Immigrants and African Americans

In Sam's words, "I grew up on the west side of Stamford, CT which was a neighborhood made up of Italian immigrants and African Americans. I've had black friends ever since I was in elementary school, especially if they played baseball or football."

In his high school years the athletic teams were integrated. At Fordham University the football team had black players. And during his two year stint with the Marines, black players were also part of the team that Sam quarterbacked.

"I just never gave race a lot of thought until the 60s when it became a major issue across the country," Sam said. "At that point it was impossible to ignore. But Al Shanen modeled himself on Paul Brown, and on his team, if you could play football you could play football, regardless of what color you were. Ask Allen Webb or Donald Goings."

Webb, a team mate of Sam's for two years on the Golden Bears before being recruited by the New York Giants of the NFL said, "It wasn't unusual for the guys on the team to go out together for a few beers after the game. Stamford as a community accepted that from athletes. By the same token, integration happened faster in sports than it did in the neighborhood. In that sense sports has historically been a catalyst for the American melting pot."

Welcome to the NFL

But when Webb was picked up by the Giants, he was introduced to a different side of America. "I remember making a trip in 1961 to play the St. Louis Cardinals – now the Arizona Cardinals – and St. Louis was south of the Mason Dixon line," Webb said.

We flew into the airport and went outside in order to go to the hotel. At this point I was informed that blacks and whites were not allowed to stay in the same hotels. So the white players all got on one bus, and the six black players got into a station wagon that escorted us to what was called *the section* – a St. Louis neighborhood where black folks resided. Rosie Grier just looked at me and said, welcome to the NFL."

Allan Webb, Stamford's ace pass defender, will be the man assigned to halt the great Bill Nickel to Joe Zack passing combination of the Flushing Vets in Boyle Stadium Sunday afternoon.

> **The NFL in 1958**
> *Jim Brown of the Cleveland Browns gained an NFL-record 1,527 yards rushing. In a divisional playoff game, the Giants held Brown to eight yards and defeated Cleveland 10-0.*

The Branch Rickey of the NFL

Paul Brown was arguably the Branch Rickey of the NFL and he was way ahead of the curve in many ways including race. For a decade after World War II Brown ignored the NFL owner's unspoken ban on black athletes with a star (white) quarterback named Otto Graham and a bruising black fullback named Marion Motley. The Browns competed in ten straight championship games, and won seven.

"If you were in the NFL and you wanted to compete with the Cleveland Browns it became harder and harder to turn down talent, even when it came in the form of a black athlete," said Webb. "Competition forced NFL owners to scrap the ban on black players and that was very influential on football teams around the nation, including the Stamford Golden Bears, and Coach Shanen who was himself a student of Paul Brown's systematic approach to football."

Webb, who hailed from neighboring Ansonia (CT), attended the University of Bridgeport where he played football and majored in Physical Education before joining Sam and the Golden Bears.

"When I graduated from college I wanted to play professional football," said Webb. "But I wasn't drafted, so I decided to stay active by playing semi-pro with the Golden Bears. That's where I met Sam, Al Shanen and a number of other players who all had legitimate shots at the NFL."

The Leader by Example

Webb remembers Sam as the undisputed leader of the Golden Bears. "Sam always played with a knee brace that Al Shanen had designed for him," Webb said. "But he led by example and not by running his mouth. He was always the first guy on the practice field, and usually the last one to leave. He was absolutely relentless when it came to coordinating with his receivers, his backs, and of course his center. Sam's work ethic rubbed off on everyone else. He made everyone around him a better player and person."

Webb speculated that the potential knee problem may have kept Sam from getting a shot with the Giants or the

Eagles. "Sam was the quarterback with a great arm who required great protection from guys like Bruno Amato and George Deenahan because of his knee. I think that Wellington Mara and Andy Robustelli may have seen a potential injury in that knee and just decided to place their bets elsewhere. A lot of athletic success is being in the right place at the right time and I was fortunate in that regard. And for whatever reason, Sam never got that shot."

Sam Had One Prejudice

"Sam Coppola had one prejudice," said Donald Goings a graduate of Stamford High, and team mate on the Golden Bears. "Sam was prejudiced against anyone who was unwilling to work at being the best that they could be. Sam was a worker himself so if you were lazy, Sam really didn't want you on his team. On the other hand, if you were willing to work at it, he didn't care if you were a Martian."

Goings and Sam both grew up on the west side of Stamford in a community that was heavily segregated with Italians in certain neighborhoods and blacks in the other neighborhoods.

"So in one sense our sporting teams were desegregated in a way that our community certainly was not," Goings said. "And it would have been very easy for Sam to be prejudiced against blacks back then, but he wasn't and I suspect that it

Don Goings, flashy Golden Bear end, will be a prime target for the aerial tosses of quarterback Sam Coppola in Sunday's game with Plainfield. Goings has been a star with the Bears since the club organized.

had everything to do with his brother JoJo. His family never sheltered JoJo. They were never ashamed of him or looked down on him in any way. And having that experience gave Sam a unique view of the world that undermined potential prejudices."

A Segregated Community

But just because Sam had avoided the trap of racial prejudice doesn't mean that blacks in Stamford did not experience it. "There were cultural limits that black people had to tolerate that started in school. In our desegregated schools there were still classes in which most students were black. And all the higher level classes were made up entirely of white students," Goings said.

"On the football team it was an unspoken fact that blacks could never aspire to be quarterbacks or centers because those positions required a level of intellect that blacks supposedly lacked. The positions of running back, defensive back, and linebacker for example were fair game. But Donovan McNabb or Michael Vick would never have been given a shot at quarterback because they'd have been considered intellectually inferior back then."

The NFL in 1963
Jim Brown of Cleveland rushed for an NFL single-season record 1,863 yards. Boston defeated Buffalo 26-8 in the first divisional playoff game in AFL history, December 28.

So as a black man back in the late fifties or early sixties it was often necessary to bite your tongue in order to avoid conflict and to get along in a society that heavily favored white folks. "This was a source of great anxiety for blacks back then and I can tell you from personal experience I often felt like there was a war going on inside my gut between the side that wanted to strike back and the side that wanted to get along," Goings said.

On the other hand, knowing guys like Sam Coppola made that tolerable for some of us back then. "Sam was a unique person in my life," said Goings. "He was always optimistic, one of those guys who succeeded at everything he tried because he didn't know he couldn't. He intuitively refused conventional indoctrinations that limited his potential. He operated outside the box and found creative solutions to problems whether on the football field or in the business community of Stamford. Sam was a quarterback in this community in many different ways," he added.

FLASHY BACKFIELD . . . These key backfield men provide a potent punch for the Stamford Golden Bears, who are running rampant over all foes this season. L-R: Leroy Vaughn, Norwalk, leading scorer; Sam Coppola, Stamford, quarterback and passer; Leroy Saylor, a halfback who is the fastest man on the squad; Bruno Amato, Stamford, fullback with five TDs to his credit; Red Altomaro, Greenwich, a defensive standout.

He Lived Life on a Higher Level

On the football field Sam was genetically gifted with a great throwing arm. But it takes lots more than being genetically gifted to become a legitimate quarterback.

"Sam took his genetic gifts and polished them relentlessly and turned himself into a great quarterback," Going said. "When he retired from football he took his business talents and polished them relentlessly and turned himself into a successful businessman."

"If Sam had decided that the NFL was his true destiny he would have made that happen too," said Goings. "Sam just lived his life on a higher level than most people, which was what I always admired most about him. I was always proud to count Sam among my friends."

During the six years that he played for them, the Golden Bears always had their share of talented black players. "Webb and Goings were two of the best. But we had a guy named LeRoy Vaughn who was an extremely talented flanker back. And LeRoy Saylor was a real solid running back. And John Kelly was outstanding at defensive tackle. And my bet is that all of these guys had dreams of making it in the NFL," Sam said.

Sam Coppola, left and John Kelly are starting players with the Stamford Golden Bears who will play the Lakeland Raiders in football in Boyle Stadium tonight, and with the Stamford Tilers, who meet the Gervasio Plumbers in the first Twi-League series game at Barrett Field Sunday morning. Coppola is quarterback and third baseman, while Kelly is a tackle and starting pitcher.

Recollections of Allen Webb

Sam also has fond recollections of Allen Webb and Donald Goings. "Allen came from the neighboring town of Ansonia, CT and was part of a high school football tradition with Stamford High that went on for years. I remember him as basically a quiet guy who was one of the best defensive backs I've ever seen. Despite the fact that he only weighed 185 pounds, when Allen Webb tackled someone, he exploded. It was like being hit by a Mack Truck," Sam said.

"He was also very capable on the offensive side of the ball and it was Allen's catching a short pass and streaking 65 yards into the end zone that set the stage for our upset victory over the Flushing Vets. I remember that play like it was yesterday," he added.

The NFL in 1966

The AFL-NFL war reached its peak, as the leagues spent a combined $7 million to sign their 1966 draft choices. The NFL signed 75 percent of its 232 draftees, the AFL 46 percent of its 181. Of the 111 common draft choices, 79 signed with the NFL, 28 with the AFL, and 4 went unsigned. Buddy Young became the first African-American to work in the league office when Commissioner Pete Rozelle named him Director of Player Relations, February 1.

Recollections of Donald Goings

"Donald Goings I remember as a natural athlete who ran like an antelope. Donald and I both grew up on the west side of Stamford so we share geographical roots. He was four or five years younger than I was, but I know he was a star at Stamford High playing both offense and defense," said Sam.

"One play that sticks out vividly in my mind involved Donald Goings catching a long pass - it must have been fifty yards or more - without missing a stride, and taking it into the end zone for a go ahead score against the Port Chester Alfonzos. But before we had a chance to celebrate, Coach Shanen spotted a flag on the field. The ref called us offside which nullified the touchdown. Regardless, that flag didn't negate the flawless beauty of Goings catching that ball in full stride and loping into the end zone. I get excited just thinking about it.

Race...on Sam's Radar

"I know that they must have experienced the entire race thing from a much different perspective than I did. But I was always proud to be playing alongside athletes and human beings the caliber of Allen Webb, Don Goings, LeRoy Vaughn, LeRoy Saylor, or John Kelly. I was always proud to call them friends and now to recall the good times we had together with the Golden Bears is wonderful. They played an important role in my life. It's not very complicated, but that was my take on race," said Sam.

8

Clippings From Sam's Scrapbook

"A picture is worth a thousand words" **A wise photographer**

Some of the Golden Bears who have been playing outstanding football as they prepare for Sunday's big Boyle Stadium contest with the Port Chester Al's. Left to right, Joe Mastropetro, line backer; Bill Kehoe, end; Don Goings, end; Sam Coppola, air-minded quarterback; Mickey Lione, kicking specialist; Luke Molloy, end; Eddie Hungaski, end, who is a defensive star; Bill Brown, tackle and end. (Walter)

One of the Golden Bear's rivals was a team from Port Chester known simply as the Alfonso's (Al's # 17 above).

Stamford Golden Bears Put Four-Game Streak

Rugged League Struggle
Fans Inter-Town Rivalry

The Stamford Golden Bears will put a four-game streak on the line for this season when they oppose the Father Alfonso Boys' Club at Corpus Christi Field, in Port Chester, Sunday at 2 p.m. The New York-Connecticut League game promises to be a hard-fought battle, with a strengthened Alfonso team looking for an upset victory to avenge the post-season exhibition defeat, 13-7, suffered at the hands of the Bears in Boyle Stadium.

Potent Starting Quartet

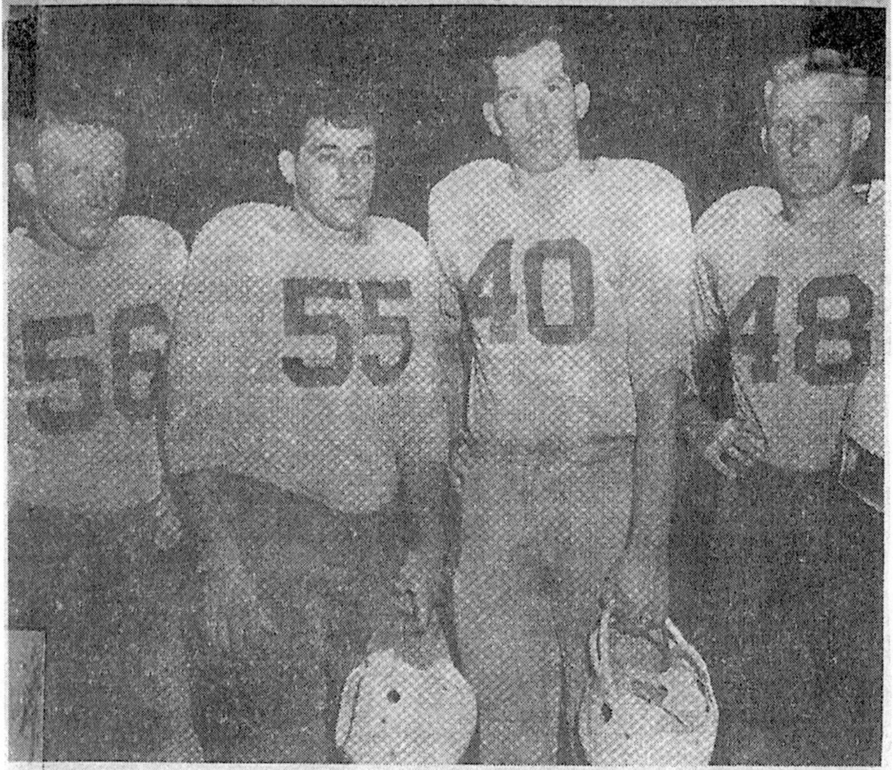

The Stamford Golden Bears will display a brilliant offensive quartet against the Port Chester Alfonsos in the big inter-county football tussle Sunday in Michael Boyle Stadium. Left to right, Red Altomaro, halfback, Bruno Amato, fullback, Sam Coppola, halfback, and Dennis Behunick, halfback.

Sam (40) depended heavily on his fullback and blocking back Bruno Amato (55), as well as his half-backs/receivers Red Altomaro (56) and Dennis Behunick (48).

Winner Of Bears-Rams Game To Claim State Semi-Pro Football Championship

Stamford Needs Clincher Victory For NY-Conn Title

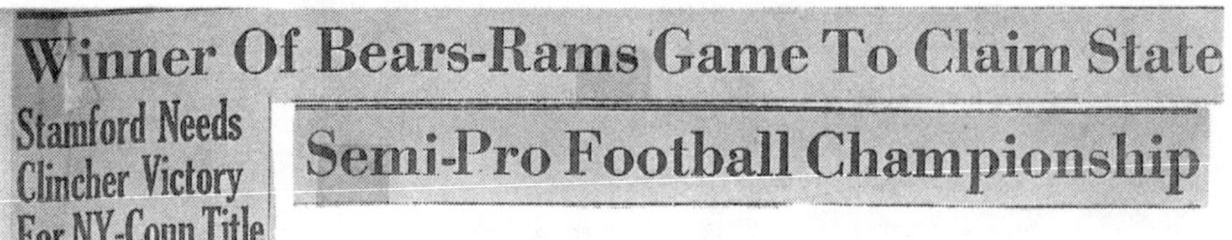

Coppola's Aerial Completions Top ACL Percentages

NEW YORK — The Providence Steamrollers and Paterson Miners,, both undefeated in the Atlantic Coast Football League to date, will seek undisputed possession of first place Saturday night, when they meet at Paterson's Hinchcliffe S t a d i u m. Frankfort plays at Ansonia in another circuit encounter, Saturday night.

The fourth-place Stamford Golden Bears will play a non-league game with the Plainfield Giants at Mount Vernon Saturday night.

Providence. a 55-0 winner over Portland last week, has three wins and one tie while Paterson has won both its league games. In the various statistical departments, the leaders are: Scoring— Willie Greenlaw, Portland; Rushing — Willie Bethea, Paterson; Passing — Jerry Morgan, Providence; Touchdown passes — Bill Baker, Paterson; Pass Receiving —Fred Denen, Providence; Punting — Ron Meyers, Paterson; Punt Returns — Jim Adams, Providence; and Kickoff returns— Tony Tavaras, Ansonia.

Stamford's Sam Coppola has turned in a sensational pass completion record in the three games in which he has played. He has passed 37 times, completing 25 for a total of 354 yards, averaging better than 14 yards per completion. His .675 plus passing percentage is tops in the league.

The standings and statistics follow:

	W.	L.	T.	Pct.
Providence	3	0	1	.1000
Paterson	2	0	0	1.000
Portland	2	2	0	.500
Stamford	2	2	1	.500
Ansonia	1	2	1	.333
Frankfort	0	4	0	.000

Sam led the Atlantic Coast Football Conference in passing percentage in every one of the ten seasons he played.

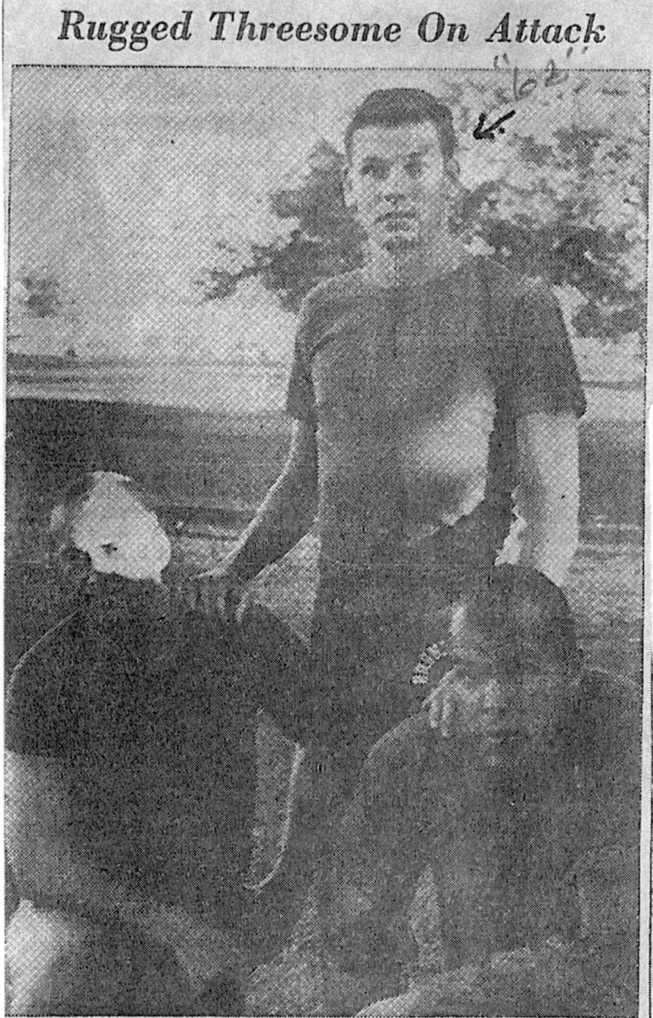

When the Stamford Golden Bears go on offense Sunday night against the Franfort-Utica entry in the Atlantic Coast League, their three men will see full time duty. Left to right, Johnny Skubel, powerful running guard, Dave Rice, a flanker back who played at Ithaca College and was with the New York Titans for a spell; and Len Rivers, the former Springfield College standout who has been a mainstay in the guard position in recent seasons.
(Walter)

Johnny Skubel (kneeling left) was a talented guard on the Bear's offense, while Dave Rice (standing) was an excellent flanker. Len Rivers (kneeling right) was one of the finest offensive linemen ever to play on the Golden Bears.

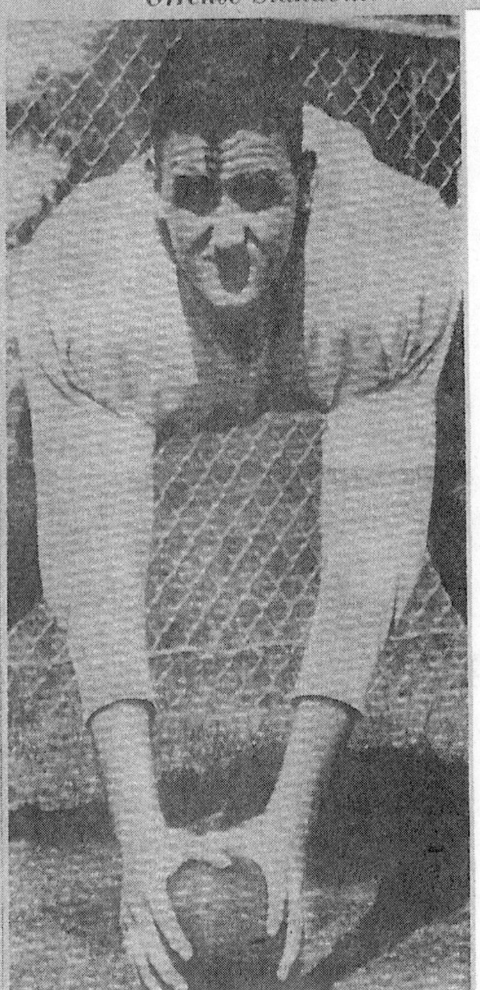

Golden Bears Seek Third-Straight

Great Neck Stadium Foe In Daylight Tilt

With predictions for fair and cool weather Sunday afternoon, another banner attendance should turn out to witness the second home exhibition test of the Golden Bears football squad in Boyle Stadium, starting at 2:30 p.m. The Bears were so convincing in their victory over West New York last Saturday night, they'll be rated as favorites to whip the Great Neck Football Club in Sunday's tussle, though the Long Island team turned in a 7-1 record against top semi-pro opposition last season.

The Bears' multiple offense received a fine sharpening under the direction of Coach Allen Shanan this week. The attack of the Stamford club appeared to be near perfection in the 40-0 victory over the Jersey club last week, but Coach Shannen pointed out flaws to his charges in this week's drills at Springdale.

With two games already under their belts, the Bears expect to be in mid-season form for Sunday's test. Promise is for a big campaign, with an exhibition triumph over the powerful Franklin, N. J., Miners, 13-6, having been registered in the opener at New Jersey two weeks ago.

New League Entry.

In Great Neck, Stamford fans will have an opportunity to witness one of three new entries in the New York - Connecticut League, which will get underway Sept. 20. The other newcomers are Brooklyn and Staten Island.

Offense Standouts With Stamford

George Deenihan was Sam's Mr. Reliable at center and a relentless blocker for 6 straight years with the Golden Bears.

George Deenihan (left), pivot man for the Golden Bears, and Luke M o l l o y, above, speedy end, will again be starters when S t a m f o r d takes possession of the ball against Great Neck in Boyle Stadium, Sunday. Both a r e former SHS star players.

Tony (Red) Altomaro is ready for big things Sunday. He will catch for the Tilers in the morning Twi-League playoff game, and provide backfield punch for the Golden Bears in the big semi-pro football game in Boyle Stadium in the afternoon. Red played halfback at Greenwich High.

Luke Malloy (left) was one of Sam's most talented receivers while Tony (Red) Altomoro (right) was one of the hardest hitting and most dependable defensive backs ever to play in the Atlantic Coast Football Conference.

Bruno Amato, the full time offensive fullback of the Golden Bears who has developed into a good placements kicker. Amato was the first man to score on the Glen Cove Vets this season, when he booted a field goal in the first quarter last Sunday which carried 35 yards over the cross bar. The former Stamford High back is prepared to join his mates in retaining the Connecticut semi-pro title at Stratford Sunday, either with his smashing thrusts into the line or as a kicking specialist.

Sam considered Bruno Amato (74) his main body-guard because he did such a great job of keeping oncoming defenders from getting to Sam and his well braced, and vulnerable left knee.

The New York Olympics will face the Stamford Golden Bears in the opening New York - Connecticut Football League game at Boyle Stadium Sunday at 2 p.m. with many former Service stars in the lineup. The team, under Coach Bob Harrington, has drawn more than the usual number of Army and Navy standouts from the Long Island area.

Interest is high in the play of the Olympics in the Flushing area. Coach Harrington reports that possibly 500 fans will accompany the Olympics to Stamford. The Olympic squad and the College Point Drum and Bugle Corps, to stage a half-time exhibition Sunday will come here by bus.

Fans Are Buzzing.

The Stamford fans are still buzzing over how the Golden Bears literally wiped up the field with the Port Chester Alphonso's in the big exhibition last Sunday. Last week's record crowd of 2,000 was pleased with the play of the home club, and another big crowd should be on hand to witness the first league contest.

Although the score was 13- against Port Chester last week the Stamford coaching staff feels that the rival goal line should have been crossed three more times.

All City Back.

John Kelly is one of the reasons why Stamford football fans are smiling these days. The former Greenwich High lineman is playing a sparkling game for the Golden Bears and will start against the N. Y. Olympics in Boyle Stadium Sunday.

John Kelly was a very talented tackle on the Golden Bears football team. He was also an excellent pitcher (along with Sam) on the Stamford Tilers twilight baseball team.

LEROY TALLIES . . . Leroy Vaughn, Norwalk, the star ball carrier of the Stamford Golden Bears, is shown on a substantial gain in a recent Boyle Stadium game. Vaughn who has a half-dozen touchdowns in five games, is given good interference by Ed Hungaski, 14, Red Altomaro, 56, Jack Leyden, 41.

LeRoy Vaughn (above) was a tough running back for the Golden Bears, and as it turned out his son Mo Vaughn became a star baseball player for the Boston Red Sox.

The defensive team of the Stamford Golden Bears has been a chief factor in the undefeated season to date. Here, the defenders take time out from a workout in preparation for Sunday's Boyle Stadium Ryan, Tony DeLuca, Bob Guerrieri, Frank Huda, Alonzo Lucas. Back row, Red Altomaro, J. B. Banks, Phil Bertuccio, Bill Wallace, Mike Potenza, Ed Hungaski. (Walter).

Defense was important even though Sam played mostly on offense. Above are some of the Golden Bears' defenders who picked up the slack when Sam came off the field.

Coach Sam Coppola of the Stamford Golden Bears backs up his team captains, Bruno Amato (left), 245-pound fullback who is reported in condition for an outstanding year, and Toto DeLuca, 255-pound defensive end. Both players have been with the Bears since they began to play football here. They'll be counted upon heavily in Sunday night's floodlight contest with the Providence Steamrollers in Boyle Stadium. The game will open Atlantic Coast Conference action for both clubs.

That's player coach Sam standing above two of his favorite team mates of all time, Bruno Amato (50) and Tito DeLuca. In Sam's opinion both had NFL potential written all over them.

Pleased With Defense

Coach Sam Coppola was more than pleased with the defensive play of his Stamford Golden Bears last Sunday night at Portland. Here, he urges four of his backfield men who had much to do with the fine work to put on the same kind of a rousing game before the home fans in Boyle Stadium Sunday night, whe nthe Franklin-Utica Falcons meet the Bears in an Atlantic Coast League game. Both clubs will be seeking initial victories in the test. Left to right, Frank Ranieri, linebacker; Hubie Hilton, wing back; Carmine Melignano, linebacker; Bob Plotkin, wing back.

(Walter)

Having played quarterback for so long, Sam (above) was comfortable coaching and calling the plays for both the Golden Bear's offensive and the defensive units.

Seven outstanding backfield holdovers from last year's great Golden Bears football team will be ready to take the gridiron when the Bears tangle with the West New York Alumni-Rec football team in an exhibition contest Saturday night at 8:30 in Michael A. Boyle Stadium. Left to right, Red Altomaro, Bill Wallace, Alan Webb, Bruno Amato, LeRoy Saylor, Sam Coppola, and LeRoy Vaughn. Webb and Amato scored touchdowns to defeat Franklin, N. Y., 13-6, last Saturday night.
(Walter)

A team practice allowed a photo to be taken of several of the Golden Bears' standouts including Bruno Amato (70), Sam, Donald Goings, Alan Webb, LeRoy Saylor, LeRoy Vaughn, and Tony (Red) Altamaro.

Sam Coppola, left, tosses short pass to Allan Webb who completes 66-yard touchdown play above. This great play occurred on Stamford's second carry in Sunday's win over the Flushing Vets. The Golden Bears were never headed thereafter. The 19-13 Stamford win ended the four-year win streak of the Vets.
(Walter)

In the biggest upset victory of Sam's career, his pass to Allan Webb (who went on to play with the NFL's N.Y. Giants) on the second play of the game produced a 66 yard touchdown jaunt and was the first straw that broke the backs and the 35 game win streak of the Flushing (Long Island) Vets.

Bears Battle Vets for Grid Le[ad]

Semi-pro football hits a peak in Stamford and Connecticut this afternoon, when the Flushing Vets, defending New York-Connecticut Semi-Pro League champions oppose the Stamford Golden Bears in Boyle Stadium starting at 1 P. M.

Both clubs are undefeated this season, in fact, the Flushing team has not been beaten in 35 consecutive games over a four-year span. The Flushing squad will be rated a favorite, though comparative scores show that Stamford has played equally as good in the current campaign.

Flushing had a tight squeeze last Sunday, defeating Port Chester 11-6. Stamford had equally as tough a time against the fired-up Port outfit on Oct. 12, winning a 13-7 decision on a pass interception by Allan Webb and 3-yard scoring aerial from quarterback Sam Coppola to Leroy Vaughn, the flashy halfback.

Flushing currently leads the circuit standings with a 6-0 record, while Stamford is 5-0. The Vets were forced into idleness for two weeks, and lost some of their edge. The 32-0 win over the Bridgeport Giants last Sunday, was won with surprising ease, however, as the previous record of the Giants did not predict a romp.

Much of Stamford's success will be dependent upon its pass de-

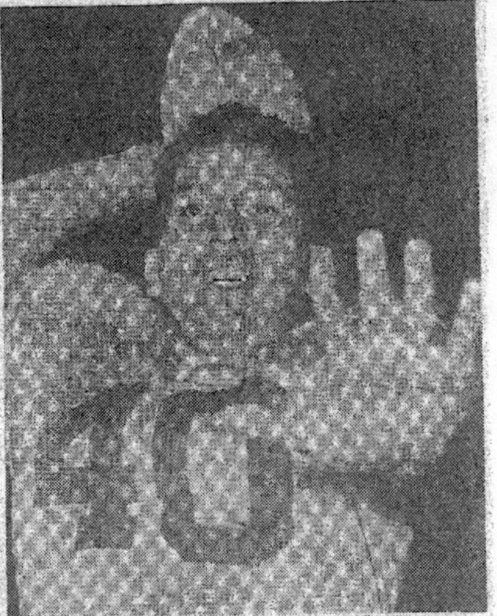

OLD RELIABLE . . . Sam Coppola, former Fordham star, is calling the plays like an old pro in his quarterback slot for the Golden Bears. He specializes in tossing forwards and will be a key man in the big game with the Flushing Vets today.

A letter from Bill Farrell, manager of the Flushing Vets, states: "One would imagine that all is well in Stamford this week and that the Golden Bears are the toast of the town, and well they should be. We thought they played a very good game Sunday and deserved to win." . . . Farrell advances the opinion that his charges believe "there certainly has been marked improvement with the Bears over last year and that it will continue." . . . Farrell is rooting for the first round playoffs in the New York - Connecticut Semi-Pro League to be Stamford against New Haven and the Vets against Port Chester. The Flushing team has changed its name to the Long Island Football Club, formerly the Flushing Football Club. . . . If Stamford enters the playoffs as scheduled, the big money would be in a game with Port Chester. That game could draw 4,000 in Boyle Stadium on a good football day.

Dynamic Golden Bears Upset Flushing 19-1[3]

Coppola's Accurate Aerials End Vets' 35-Game Streak

Quarterback Sam Coppola pitched three scoring passes as the Stamford Golden Bears ended the 35-game streak of the Flushing Vets with a 19-13 triumph before more than 2,000 howling fans in Boyle Stadium Sunday afternoon. Coppola, a baseball pitcher of ability, never chucked better as he sparked the Bears to the seventh straight win of the season. With the upset success, Stamford took over the lead in the New York-Connecticut Semi-Pro League.

Stamford now has a 6-0 league record, while Flushing is 6-1.

Hold Firm.

Carrying a tremendous weight advantage, Flushing struck for two quick first downs after taking the opening kickoff. But the Bears held firm, forcing the visitors to punt, the ball going out of bounds on the Stamford 32.

The first Stamford tally came with such stunning quickness that it electrified the crowd. After Bruno Amato plunged for two yards, Coppola tossed a short pass to halfback Allan Webb, who took the ball on the line of scrimmage, cut to the outside and then zigzagged to pick up three blockers and went all the way for a 60-yard scoring play. Webb's speed dazzled the defenders on the brilliant sortie.

Final Surge.

After tackle Alonzo Lucas recovered a Flushing fumble on the Vets' 36 in the third quarter, Stamford struck for its final score. A Coppola-to-Keough pass provided a first down on the 27. Coppola shot a bullet over the middle to Goings for six yards. With second down on the 24, Coppola hit Leroy Vaughn on the goal line. The Stamford club's leading scorer with eight touchdowns brushed the flag marking the sideline as he went into pay dirt.

Litchard's boot was true for the extra point and Stamford converted to take a 19-6 lead.

The Vets, realizing that something heroic was needed to stem the tide, took the ensuing kickoff and carried from its own 34 for a score. The tally was made on a 13-yard aerial gain from Nickel to Bill Meldau. Trupo added the extra point.

Penalties Hurt.

The 1958 Stamford Golden Bears. Sam is # 40 in the back row.

THE SCORE
By MAURICE "MOE" MAGLIOLA

We've had so many people ask for an explanation of the DRAW PLAY, because of our use of the term in describing the play of the Stamford Golden Bears, that it may be enlightening if a glossary of football terms were presented here. The Bears used the play with tremendous success in the early season, with Bruno Amato the ball carrier. The DRAW PLAY is used in a passing situation, drawing the opposing lineman into the offensive backfield. The passer fades back, then hands off to a teammate who hits hard up the middle. Here are some other terms: UMBRELLA DEFENSE—Zone-type aerial defense with two deep defenders and two halfbacks usually playing out wide ... BELLY SERIES—Group of plays from "T" formation in which the quarterback places the ball in a teammate's possession in the stomach area. He may leave ball with player, or fake it and then take it away. ... BOOTLEG—Quarterback, or other ball carrier, fakes giving ball to a teammate, hides ball on his hip, and runs without blocking in opposite direction. The Bears' Sam Coppola has completely baffled the opposition with such a play at times this season. Fans here will never forget how completely he foiled the Port Chester defense, only to have a wide-open receiver allow the leather to slip through his fingers over the goal line. ... CLIPPING — Running or diving into the back, or throwing the body across the back of the leg of an opponent not carrying the ball is illegal. The penalty is 15 yards and is one which stops more scoring plays than any other assessment.

Moe Magliola was a legendary sportswriter for the Stamford Advocate. He covered the Golden Bears and the Stamford Tilers for the entire decade during which Sam played.

The Silent Quarterback

Brother JoJo

"The moral test of government is how it treats those who are in the dawn of life . . . the children; those who are in the twilight of life . . . the elderly; and those who are in the shadow of life . . . the sick . . . the needy . . . and the disabled." . . . **Hubert Humphrey**

Joseph (JoJo) Coppola didn't have a 90 mph fastball when he was 15 years old like his younger brother Sam. He also didn't have the ability to knock baseballs out of the ball park on a regular basis like his youngest brother Mike. In fact you could easily define JoJo according to all the things he didn't have which included any formal education, so he could never read or write.

JoJo was born on November 29, 1928, a year before the stock market crash that started the Great Depression, to Mike and Eva Coppola. In those days C-sections were not a part of the medical doctor's repertoire. So when he was ready to be born JoJo was forced out with the help of forceps. In the process he sustained a head injury that prevented him from mentally developing beyond the age of six.

Things JoJo Didn't Have

JoJo didn't have any of the athletic skills and experiences that both of his younger brothers had. He never had a conventional job. He never had his own money. And he never had relations with a woman.

JoJo had no real interest in sports. Instead he preferred watching the Three Stooges, Roy Rogers, and of course the one and only Lone Ranger and his trusty Indian companion Tonto. Jo spent a high percentage of his waking hours sitting in front of his TV and he knew every detail about his favorite shows. When interacting with his brothers or his parents, TV topics inevitably made up large parts of the conversation.

Things JoJo Did Have

On the other hand, for all the shortcomings that he experienced in life, there were some important things that he did have, starting with parents who cared very deeply for him and did everything in their power to make sure that JoJo's shortcomings were accommodated for in a multitude of ways. He also had two younger brothers who made it their business to make sure Jo's life was as meaningful as it could be.

"I'd quiz him," said Sam. "I'd say what's the name of Roy Roger's horse, and without hesitation Jo would answer Trigger. I'd say who's Roy Roger's wife and Jo would answer Dale Evans. He always took pride in being able to come up with those answers quickly," Sam said.

JoJo Knew What He Knew

Although Jo lived a relatively uncomplicated life, there were some important things of which he was well aware. JoJo knew when he was happy and he knew when he was unhappy, and he didn't hide either from anyone. He also knew when he was hungry and he ate. He knew when he was tired and he'd go to sleep. "In those ways Jo was smarter than me," Sam said. "I wish I'd always been smart enough to eat when I was hungry and sleep when I was tired."

Experiences at Southbury Training School

One of the difficulties that came with a mentally challenged son was the fact that JoJo was unable to control his bowels, which caused Eva and Mike Sr. a lot of extra work. At one point, when JoJo was in his early teens, a friend suggested that Mike and Eva should consider sending Jo to Southbury Training School where they had medical experts who knew how to work with kids like JoJo and could help him learn to control his bowels.

The NFL in 1943
Slingin' Sammy Baugh led the league in passing, punting, and interceptions. He led the Washington Redskins to a tie with the New York Giants for the Eastern Division title, and then to a 28-0 victory in a divisional playoff game. The Bears beat the Redskins 41-21 in the NFL Championship Game, December 26, 1943.

After several weeks of serious reflection, Eva and Mike Sr. decided in favor of taking JoJo to Southbury in order to see if the problem could be resolved.

"Jo was in Southbury Training School for the better part of three years," said Sam. "That's how long it took them to help JoJo overcome his problem. But during those three years my mom would pack up a picnic lunch, my dad would gather up Mike and me, and we'd all drive over to Southbury every other week in order to spend several hours with Jo."

After a while cousins and friends joined in and Mike Sr. and Eva did everything they could do to make Jo's time away from home comfortable."

"Once the problem was resolved my dad made arrangements to bring him home, and I'll never forget that the people from Southbury paid us a couple of visits a month to make sure that Jo was on track. That went on for six months until they knew everything was OK," Sam said.

When he arrived back home JoJo was 5' 7" tall and weighed a good 160 pounds. He was gentle and he loved to laugh and to make other people laugh. On the other hand, he didn't like anyone laughing at him. Sam and Mike Jr. saw to it that nobody was making fun of their brother JoJo.

When JoJo Went to Work

"JoJo always occupied a special place in our family." said Mike Jr. "When my dad was alive he took Jo to work several times each week and gave him chores that he could perform, and along with those chores came some dignity that he would have otherwise lacked. My dad understood that and he made it a point to include JoJo whenever possible."

The Orange Soda Kid

JoJo was often invited to accompany his dad or his brothers when they were going over to the local tap. "All the locals knew JoJo and would go out of their way to make sure that his glass was full of orange soda, which was his favorite drink," said Sam. "In Jo's case his glass was always at least half full because of all the friends he'd made when we'd take him over to the tap.

He also had a collection of hats and magazines that he picked up around town. "Despite the fact that he couldn't read or write a word, he loved all the photos. If we were in the dentist's office for example and JoJo spotted a magazine that wasn't nailed down, he wasn't shy about asking the secretary if he could have it," said Sam. "And most of the time they'd accommodate him with a smile."

Eddie Broadhurst

An unexpected result of Jo's time at Southbury Training School was that Millie learned about one of Sam's cousins who had a son who'd fallen out of a second story window, sustained brain damage, and was getting his rehabilitation at Southbury, just like Jo had done. "I was introduced to this young fellow named Ed Broadhurst and I was so impressed that I told the school I wanted to hire him to work at Stamford Tile."

The NFL in 1950

*The Los Angeles Rams became the first NFL team to have all of its games - both home and away - **TELEVISED**. The Washington Redskins followed the Los Angeles Rams in arranging to televise their games. Other teams made deals to put selected games on television. Cleveland defeated Los Angeles 30-28 in the NFL Championship Game, December 24, 1950.*

Sam signed the necessary papers, brought him home, and put Ed to work. "Like JoJo, Eddie had never learned to read and write, but I discovered that he was a ferocious and dedicated worker, and he ended up working for Stamford Tile for 40 years, eventually supporting a wife and two kids," Sam said. "He always called me Boss."

There was one occasion when Sam had negotiated a particularly good real estate deal, and in the wake he went to the bank, withdrew ten new $100 dollar bills, he drove over to their house and presented Eddie and his wife with the money. "Ed asked what the money was for. I just said it was a bonus for being such a great worker," said Sam. "I knew that extra money was going to come in handy."

Jo Was Devastated

In 1961 when Mike Sr. passed away, JoJo was devastated. He was unhappy and everyone knew it. "It was if he'd lost his best friend," said Sam. "He had a real hard time understanding what happened and why. He had a real hard time letting go, but in the end, like everyone else, Jo survived the storm with the help of Ma, Sam, and me," said Mike Jr.

Not long afterwards Sam bought a smaller house for Ma and JoJo. Eva did everything in her power to help Jo.

"But there were things that Ma was physically incapable of doing," said Sam. "Jo was mentally only six years old, but he weighed as much as a normal 30 year old man, and for Ma to wrestle him in and out of the shower for example, was just too much. So Mike and I stepped in and started taking over some of those more challenging duties."

That labor of love continued for over three decades when Sam and Mike finally had to find a nursing home for Ma, and JoJo moved in with Sam and Millie. "Millie was always great with Jo," Sam said. "She washed his clothes, cooked for him, brought his meals to him, and generally treated him like her own son. Predictably, Jo's favorite part of any meal was desert, whether it was ice cream, pie, or a cookie. JoJo loved anything sweet."

Petrina, Sam's youngest daughter developed a special relationship with Joseph. "He was so excited when she got married and he wanted to see all the photos," Sam said. "Unfortunately he was in a wheelchair by that time and was unable to attend the ceremony. But to the very end Jo and Petrina had a deep appreciation for one another."

Ma Coppola passed away in 1993 at age 86. JoJo lived until 2003 when he passed on at age 75. The parameters of JoJo's life were narrow and limited when compared to the rest of his family. By the same token, his limitations and his warm personality had profound effects on his mother, his father, as well as both of his brothers, Sam and Mike Jr.

JoJo and Petrina

> **The NFL in 1955**
> *The Baltimore Colts made an 80-cent phone call to Johnny Unitas and signed him as a free agent. Another quarterback, Otto Graham, played his last game as the Cleveland Browns defeated the L.A. Rams 38-14 in the NFL Championship Game, December 26. Graham quarterbacked the Browns to 10 championship-game appearances in 10 years, and won 7.*

JoJo in Contrast

In simplest terms, Sam and Mike Jr. had always been naturally talented athletes. They were the captains of the team, or the first ones chosen on the playground when teams were picked. They were physically superior and they carried themselves with a level of confidence that physical superiority naturally generates.

JoJo on the other hand was never chosen for any team on any playground. He never made it to the playground, and as such he lived a profoundly different life than his two athletically talented brothers.

And it was this stark contrast with JoJo that gave both Sam and Mike Jr. a unique sense of humility that's often lacking in highly talented athletes. They were both painfully aware of the fact that everyone was not born with the same tool box to work with. They knew first hand that winning is not always a matter of applying oneself fully.

Thanks to JoJo, Sam and Mike Jr. understood first hand that there are people in this world who need a little more help than others. They also understood first hand that there are unique benefits and payoffs for helping those who need it.

Sam's Take on Enlightened Self Interest

Due to his experiences with JoJo as well as his experiences on the football field and the baseball diamond, Sam developed his own athletic take on the concept known as enlightened self interest.

"On the football field there was never any doubt in my mind that if Bruno Amato got hurt, I was in trouble. So I knew for sure that what was good for Bruno was good for me," Sam said. "What was good for my center George Deenahan was good for me. What was good for my receivers was good for me. We all looked out after each other."

"This was a one for all, all for one orientation to the game which recognized that if done right, the whole was greater than the sum of its parts. It was synergy. It was teamwork. And in philosophical circles that idea is known as enlightened self interest, in contrast to a me first, greedy, unenlightened self interest," said Sam. "Life is a team game."

JoJo

Kelly Coppola is Sam's daughter in law (Tommy's wife) who held JoJo in such high regard that when he passed away she wrote the following poem in his memory.

OUR SPECIAL JOE

ASK HIM THE NAME OF THAT HORSE KNOWN AS TRIGGER,
FOR HIS LOVE OF THE MOVIES, NO FAN WAS MUCH BIGGER,
OR QUIZ HIM ON QUESTIONS ABOUT THE OLD SHOWS,
THE STOOGES OR TONTO, THE LONE RANGERS "HI-HO'S"
FOR THE MOVIES BROUGHT SMILES UPON HIS SWEET FACE,
AS HE DID FOR US, AT ONE STEADY PACE.

WHETHER HE ASKED FOR A BUCK, (OR PROBABLY TWO)
OR SHOWED YOU A FLASHLIGHT, (WHICH HE KEPT QUITE A FEW)
HIS FACE STAYED SO INNOCENT, HIS HEART FULL OF LOVE,
WHICH NOW WILL SPREAD SUNSHINE FROM "SOMEWHERE" ABOVE.

HE'D TELL YOU THAT MASTIC, "OUT WEIGHED" THE CEMENT,
OR DOWN THE DRAIN- IS WHERE HIS "HAIR" WENT,
OR WHY HE'D NEVER DRIVE IN A CAR WITH THAT "SANTO",
OR HOW HE'D HANG OUT WITH "TALIAN" OR WITH GEE-JOE.

ON HIS TRAVELS HE'D POP IN ON PELLICCIS AND SNAKE,
AND LEGATO'S FOR MAGAZINES WHERE "TWO" HE WOULD TAKE.

FIX HIM A PLATE OF MEATBALLS WITH SPAGHETTI, ORANGE SODA OR
PANCAKES, OF WHICH HE ATE PLENTY!

HIS HUGS THEY WERE SPECIAL- THE TIGHTER THE BETTER,
"WHAT'S YOUR NAME?" "DO YOU LIKE ME?" WAS HIS VERBAL HEADER.
OR WHAT HOW HIS SMILE COULD WARM YOU INSIDE,
FOR GENTLE AND HEARTFELT HIS TRAITS COULD NOT HIDE.

SO NOW JOE, MOVE ON, JOIN OLD FAMILY/FRIENDS TOO
FOR IN LIFE WE STILL ASK, "WHO HAD IT BETTER THAN YOU?"

GOD SPARED YOU LIFE'S HARDSHIPS- YOU WERE GIFTED THATS HOW,
AS FOR THE PAIN AND EXHAUSTION, WE CAN HEAR YOU WHISPER,
"NO MORE NOW"

KELLY COPPOLA
5/11/2004

The Sam Coppola Baseball League

"Baseball is a game where a curve is an optical illusion, a screwball can be a pitch or a person, stealing is legal, and you can spit anywhere you like except in the umpire's eye or on the ball."
Jim Murray

It's as American as baseball, motherhood, and apple pie. How many times have you heard that familiar phrase? Of course every kid deserves to have a good mom. In moderation, every kid deserves to have an occasional slice of Mom's scrumptious, 4th of July apple pie.

And in the eyes of Sam Coppola, every kid also deserves the opportunity to dig in at the plate, wait for the pitcher to deliver the ol' ball, and then to rip it into the outfield for a single, a double, a triple, or even a home run. That is to say, any kid who's denied the opportunity to play baseball is being denied an important piece of his or her red, white, and blue heritage as far as Sam was concerned.

How to Accommodate All Those Kids?

In the spring of 1975 Sam was running errands one afternoon when the local Babe Ruth League was holding baseball tryouts for kids ages 13 to 15 at Stamford High's baseball field. As he was passing by he decided to pull into the school's parking lot. He got out of his car, walked over to the field, and proceeded to watch for a half an hour or so.

Sitting in the bleachers Sam recognized one of the coaches, a guy named Mickey Leone that he'd known for years. When Mickey walked over to say hello, Sam asked what he was going to do with all those kids. There were well over a hundred, and Mickey confessed they'd be unable to accommodate more than a handful, so most would be turned away. In other words, lots of kids were being denied an opportunity to play baseball. To Sam that was un-American.

Disappointment Translates Into Action

"The next day I called a friend named Dick Mollo who worked for the City of Stamford and who had all kinds of valuable connections around the area. I asked Dick to meet me at the Dubby's tap so I could tell him about a problem I'd encountered the day before," Sam said.

Sam told Mollo about the comments made by Coach Leone and how disappointed he'd been to learn that so many local kids were being deprived of the opportunity to play baseball, an experience that Sam himself had found profoundly valuable during his own growing up years.

"My heart just went out to all those kids. Without baseball what will they have to look forward to this summer? Three months of thumb twiddling? I think we should do something about this potential problem. What's in the realm of possibility," Sam asked.

> **The NFL in 1976**
> *Pittsburgh defeated Dallas 21-17 in Super Bowl X in Miami. The Steelers joined Green Bay and Miami as the only teams to win two Super Bowls; the Cowboys became the first wild-card team to play in the Super Bowl. The CBS telecast was viewed by an estimated 80 million people, which was to date the largest television audience in history.*

Let's Start a New League

Mollo thought for a moment before suggesting that they could start an alternative league for all those kids who failed to make the Babe Ruth League team. Sam said he thought that was a great idea, but he was up to his eyeballs with his business at the moment. "But I know plenty of people in the business community," Sam said, "and I'd be willing to recruit sponsors to buy uniforms and equipment."

Mollo said that through his connections he could arrange for the new league to have access to an area field or two. He also said that the local Italian American Association had a nice room in which they could hold some board meetings if they had board members who wanted to meet and organize a new league.

"Over the next several months Dick and I began putting the pieces of the new league together," Sam said. "I knew several members of the business community who had the right age kids and who'd be willing to serve on our board. Dick arranged for us to hold hour meetings at the Italian American Association's meeting room, and we were off and running with what we originally named the Italian American Youth Baseball League."

The Sunday Post

Section C.

Sam Coppola gave kids a chance to play baseball

I didn't want to see any kid walk away rejected.

— Sam Coppola

By CLAUDE DIXON

STAMFORD — They're coming from throughout the area and as far away as Florida to say goodby to Sam Coppola at his going-away testimonial dinner tonight at the Italian Center.

"I'm completely overwhelmed by the whole thing," said Coppola, former Marine, star quarterback on the one-time award-winning Golden Bears semi-pros football team, and founder of the Sam Coppola 13-15 year old Baseball League. "It's a tremendous honor to have your friends do something like this for you."

WHY IS Sam being honored?

The reasons are as many as the number of people, some 300 are expected, who will attend the affair which starts at six o'clock.

"Some will be honoring Sam for his

sandlots and football on city streets.

"When night came, and the lights went on a long Spruce Street, was when my friends and I started our games," he said.

HE WAS 12 at the time and football was to remain a passion with him through high school, college, the services and his years with the Golden Bears.

"I went to St. Basil's Prep and played all sports including baseball, football and track," he said. "I did the same at Eastern Military Academy which used to be here in Stamford."

Coppola graduated from the academy in 1947 and spent a post-graduate year at Carteret High School in New Jersey where he was captain of the football team, played baseball, and was elected school president.

"The competition was heavy that year," he said. "The school's schedule included freshmen college teams such as the plebes from the U.S. Military Academy."

one deserved to be in the league's Hall of Fame, it's Sam Coppola himself, and tonight, as those 300 gather to say hello and goodby to Sam, that's what will happen.

GOODBY SAM — Sam Coppola, founder of Sam Coppola Baseball, a league formed to give kids rejected by Babe Ruth League teams a chance to play ball, will be given a going-away testimonial dinner tonight at the Italian Center in Stamford. Below, Coppola, left, is shown at opening day of the 1979 season which was rained out at Cuberta Stadium. That's Dick Mollo, league commissioner with him, and Jane Hurley, Miss Sam Coppola 1979 and Miss Greater Stamford, they're trying to shield from the rain. (Recent Coppola Photo by Gene Connolly.)

Brick by Brick

The new group (including board members Lois Cammerota, Joseph Columbo, Richard Molgano, Robert LiBrandi, Ralph Martin, Anita DeLeo, Donald Donohue Jr, and Frank Cicero) initially started meeting once a week. But soon they increased to twice a week over the next year, and brick by brick the new league was organized. "It was amazing how many details were involved in putting a project like this together," said Sam. "And knowing how busy I was - with all the balls I was juggling - Dick covered 90% of the details from recruiting coaches to scheduling tryouts."

Fundraising was one top priority, and in order to cover all those bases the new group asked the community to get involved in a variety of ways. They had bake-sales, pizza sales, and to top it off they decided to raffle off a new car.

"I went to a local auto dealer, bought a brand new Toyota Corolla for $2900 (this was 1975), and the group proceeded to sell boatloads of tickets at $5 a head," Sam said. "That raffle, in conjunction with the sponsors buying uniforms and equipment for those kids who were on their sponsored team, paid for most everything," he added.

No Player Left Behind

Dick Mollo did some advertising in the Stamford Advocate, and in early April of '76 the brand new Italian American Baseball League held their first tryouts. Coaches scouted the talent, made their selections, handed out the uniforms, and scheduled practices.

"We held our tryouts a week after the Babe Ruth League held theirs so we'd avoid any conflicts," Sam said. "Most importantly, we didn't leave one kid out in the cold, which was the primary goal of this new endeavor," said Sam. "Dick and I were both proud of how that worked out."

Mayor Louis Clapps Spoke

The first week in May an official kick-off celebration was held and lots of dignitaries were invited to participate including Mayor Louis Clapps, Senator William E. Strada, and local sports radio personality Len Gambino. Mayor

Clapps not only showed up, but he delivered an eloquent speech that was very complimentary to our entire group, and it was an important part of what made this event so memorable for everyone who attended," said Sam.

Pulling a Daughter-in-law Out of the Hat

"Part of the kick-off ceremony was the raffle drawing, and my youngest son Tommy, age 9 at the time, was asked to stick his hand into the container, swirl it around a few times, and pick out the winner," Sam said.

Tom swirled his hand around several times and pulled out the name Joe Santagata. Joe was a guy who Sam had known from the tile business and he was absolutely ecstatic to find out that he was the winner of a brand new car.

"Ironically," Sam said "fifteen years later Tommy began dating Joe's daughter Kelly and in 1989 Tommy and Kelly were married, so she's now my daughter in law. It's a small world," he added.

In 1976, with ten teams competing, the Italian American Baseball League was launched, and they proceeded to have an incredibly wonderful initial season.

The NFL in 1980

Television ratings in 1980 were the second-best in NFL history, trailing only the combined ratings of the 1976 season. All three networks posted gains, and NBC's 15.0 rating was its best ever. CBS and ABC had their best ratings since 1977, with 15.3 and 20.8 ratings, respectively. CBS Radio reported a record audience of 7 million for Monday night games.

"Each team had 15 or 16 players," Sam said, "so we gave over 150 kids a chance to play ball who would otherwise have no chance. There was only one glitch in the entire season, and it came at the end. We challenged the Babe Ruth League to an All Star Game under the lights. They took us up on it and proceeded to beat the daylights out of our kids. But as you'll see, we'd get our revenge a couple of seasons later.

Otherwise things went down as smooth as silk, primarily because of Dick Mollo."

Surprise, Surprise

They spent the off season planning and polishing season one's experiences. But in the background Dick Mollo was making some other plans to which Sam was not privy to until opening day.

Dick had publicized the event and had invited local dignitaries to give the appropriate send off. Just before Dick made the introductions he said he had an announcement to make.

"At that point he told the crowd that the board had decided to rename the league after me." Sam said. "I almost fainted on the spot. But thanks to Dick Mollo and the rest of the board members who planned this thing in secret, from that point forward all our teams took the field under the Sam Coppola Baseball League flag. I was absolutely stunned," Sam added.

An Official Sam Coppola League Uniform

Grand Marshall Joe DiMaggio

In year three (1978) Dick Mollo decided that we should hold a carnival for our big annual fund raiser. He also had an acquaintance named John DiPoli who was good friends with Joe DiMaggio – the legendary Yankee Clipper, who by then was a couple of decades into retirement. DiPoli thought he might be able to get DiMaggio to act as the Grand Marshall of the carnival. Mollo knew that would draw a huge crowd.

"A month before the event we heard that the connection had been made and that DiMaggio had agreed to be The Sam Coppola Baseball League's Grand Marshall. When the day arrived Joe came early and was the most accommodating celebrity I'd ever met," said Sam. "Despite the fact that he had a little cold, Joe shook hands with everyone, gave a very supportive presentation to the crowd. He spent most of the day with our group and everyone had DiMaggio fever for several weeks after that event."

Grand Marshall Joe DiMaggio

Beating the Babe Ruth All Stars

Every season The Sam Coppola League named an All Star team and they competed unsuccessfully against the local Babe Ruth League up until 1980. "By that season, though, we were starting to get kids who intentionally by-passed the Babe Ruth League in order to play in the Sam Coppola League," said Sam. "By 1980 everyone thought we finally had the talent to compete with our arch-rivals. I don't recall many details but I do remember that we had a young lefty named John who pitched a great game, and we won 8 to7 in a real nail biter," Sam said. "Our kids were so proud of themselves they couldn't stop smiling for weeks."

The Orange Crushed

Prior to the 1981 game between the Sam Coppola All Stars and their coaches, Sam decided to paint an orange white and to have Millie paint laces on it in order to make it look like a baseball. In the middle of the game, with Sam on the mound, and Mollo behind the plate one of the coaches came out and slipped the orange to Sam.

"One of our best hitters was at the plate and I served him up a pitch that he couldn't refuse. He made solid contact and that white orange splashed all over the batter and Dick Mollo. The whole place was in tears for five minutes before we resumed the game," said Sam. I'll never forget the look on his face when he realized that he'd smashed an orange instead of a baseball."

One Quick Word About Dick Mollo

"Dick Mollo," in Sam's words, "was a non-stop organizer and fund raiser. One year for example, he arranged for our coaches to play an exhibition softball game against a dozen Playboy models who came over to help us raise funds."

Coppola & Mollo at exhibition game

"On another occasion he arranged for our coaches to play a baseball game against the Sam Coppola All Stars. We always had a great time, always got great press, and raised some great money all at the same time. There were so many times I wished the board had named it the Sam Coppola/ Dick Mollo League," Sam said. "This project would never have seen the light of day without Dick Mollo's artful touch."

The Curtain Finally Falls on Success

By 1981, with six successful seasons under their belt, both Sam and Dick thought that their new league was detracting too much from the Babe Ruth League, which they didn't intend for it to do. With that thought in mind they announced that 1981 would be their final season of operation.

In order to celebrate the closing as well as their successes, Mollo decided that they needed to organize a closing event in the honor of the guy after whom the league was named. Dick arranged for Senator William E. Strada to be the honorary chairman of a classy banquet scheduled to be held at the Italian Center Hall in a room that held 250 guests.

"Dick, the board members, as well as committee members Charles Magyar, Dennis Behunick, Joseph Zezima, Jim Hickey, Michael Coppola, and Tony Romano did a marvelous job in promoting the event," Sam said, "and they sold the whole thing out at $25 per ticket. He kept me and my family in a back room until everyone was seated. When I came out I was given a standing ovation. I know my face must have been a bright red," Sam said.

"While everyone was clapping I made it a point to walk around to each table and shake the hand of each and every attendee. I was flattered beyond belief. Dick introduced me and handed the microphone over to me and I proceeded to thank all the people and kids who'd played a role in the success of Sam Coppola Baseball."

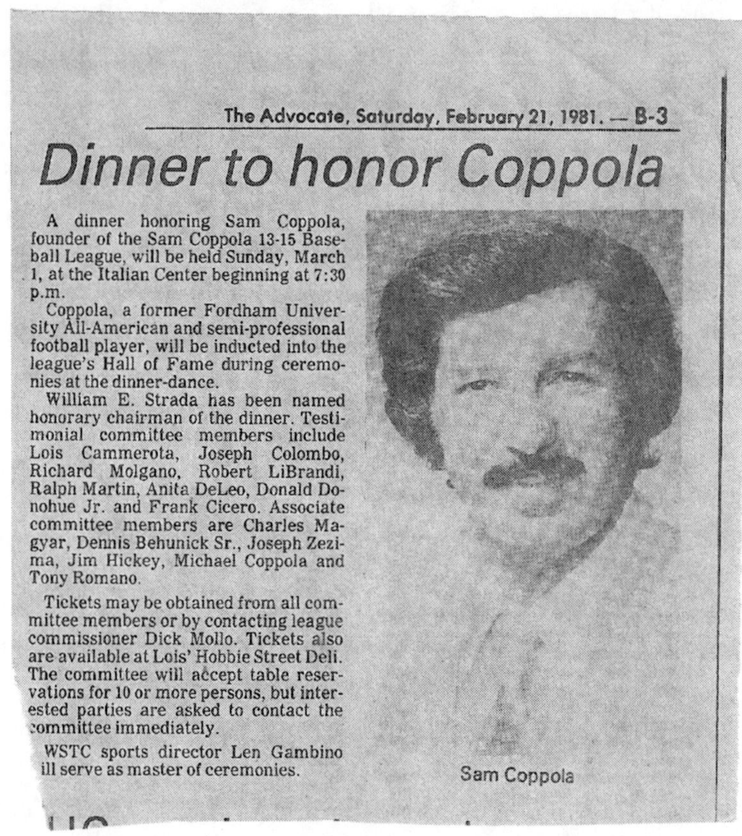

The Advocate, Saturday, February 21, 1981. — B-3

Dinner to honor Coppola

A dinner honoring Sam Coppola, founder of the Sam Coppola 13-15 Baseball League, will be held Sunday, March 1, at the Italian Center beginning at 7:30 p.m.

Coppola, a former Fordham University All-American and semi-professional football player, will be inducted into the league's Hall of Fame during ceremonies at the dinner-dance.

William E. Strada has been named honorary chairman of the dinner. Testimonial committee members include Lois Cammerota, Joseph Colombo, Richard Molgano, Robert LiBrandi, Ralph Martin, Anita DeLeo, Donald Donohue Jr. and Frank Cicero. Associate committee members are Charles Magyar, Dennis Behunick Sr., Joseph Zezima, Jim Hickey, Michael Coppola and Tony Romano.

Tickets may be obtained from all committee members or by contacting league commissioner Dick Mollo. Tickets also are available at Lois' Hobbie Street Deli. The committee will accept table reservations for 10 or more persons, but interested parties are asked to contact the committee immediately.

WSTC sports director Len Gambino ill serve as master of ceremonies.

Sam Coppola

Governor O'Neil Adds the Final Touch

One dignitary that Dick invited but who was unable to attend was then Governor Bill O'Neil. "In lieu of his attendance, Dick capped off the evening by presenting me with a beautiful letter of commendation written and signed by the Governor himself," Sam said. "I was so moved and flattered that I framed the letter the next day and I've kept it on my office wall ever since."

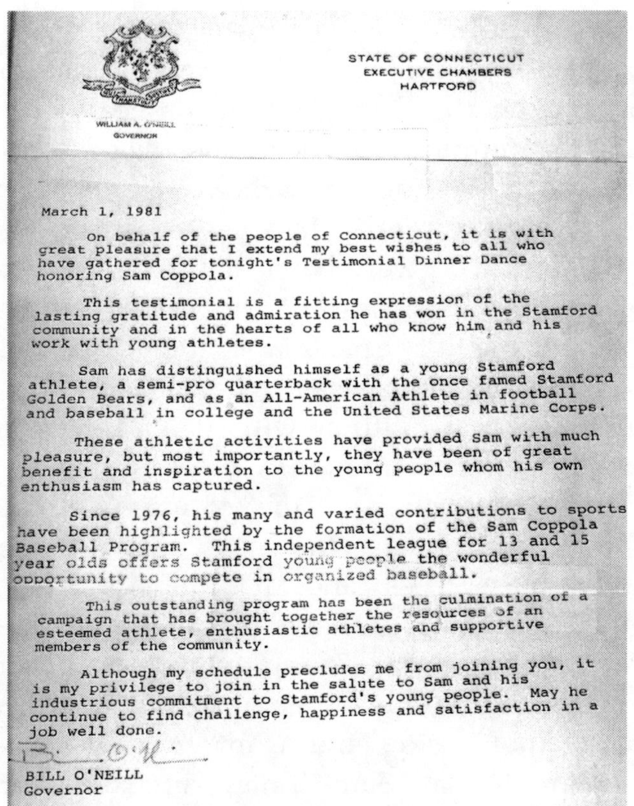

STATE OF CONNECTICUT
EXECUTIVE CHAMBERS
HARTFORD

WILLIAM A. O'NEILL
GOVERNOR

March 1, 1981

On behalf of the people of Connecticut, it is with great pleasure that I extend my best wishes to all who have gathered for tonight's Testimonial Dinner Dance honoring Sam Coppola.

This testimonial is a fitting expression of the lasting gratitude and admiration he has won in the Stamford community and in the hearts of all who know him and his work with young athletes.

Sam has distinguished himself as a young Stamford athlete, a semi-pro quarterback with the once famed Stamford Golden Bears, and as an All-American Athlete in football and baseball in college and the United States Marine Corps.

These athletic activities have provided Sam with much pleasure, but most importantly, they have been of great benefit and inspiration to the young people whom his own enthusiasm has captured.

Since 1976, his many and varied contributions to sports have been highlighted by the formation of the Sam Coppola Baseball Program. This independent league for 13 and 15 year olds offers Stamford young people the wonderful opportunity to compete in organized baseball.

This outstanding program has been the culmination of a campaign that has brought together the resources of an esteemed athlete, enthusiastic athletes and supportive members of the community.

Although my schedule precludes me from joining you, it is my privilege to join in the salute to Sam and his industrious commitment to Stamford's young people. May he continue to find challenge, happiness and satisfaction in a job well done.

BILL O'NEILL
Governor

Governor O'Neil's Letter

"Everything came off beautifully and to this day I can't say enough about Dick Mollo who was the real driving force behind the league. He was always giving me credit for things that he'd really done himself. But that's how Dick Mollo worked," Sam said.

> **The NFL in 1981**
> *Regular-season attendance-13.6 million, averaged 60,745-set a record for the fourth year in a row. It also was the first time the per-game average exceeded 60,000. NFL games in 1981 were played before 93.8 percent of total stadium capacity. ABC and CBS set all-time rating highs. ABC finished with a 21.7 rating and CBS with a 17.5 rating. NBC was down slightly to 13.9.*

What Motivated Sam?

To this day Sam still contemplates the motivation behind organizing the Sam Coppola Baseball League. "We had continual community support whenever we asked for it. But the more I think about this whole experience the more I realize that it was my brother Joseph who caused me to have empathy for kids who were being denied an opportunity to play baseball on that spring afternoon back in 1975," Sam said. "JoJo made me fully appreciate people, especially kids."

The other influence was my sporting experiences in which no game meant anything without a level playing field," said Sam. "Whether you're on a football field, a baseball diamond, or a basketball court, the score always starts at zero to zero. You have officials who make sure that everyone is playing within the rules, and that nobody has an unfair advantage. This in turn makes the competition meaningful. When I see people who are being denied an opportunity, or people who are taking advantage of others, it strikes a nerve in my brain that makes me want to stand up and do something about it," said Sam. "Enter Sam Coppola Baseball."

Sam Coppola
58 Anderson Street,
Stamford, Connecticut

May 27, 1977

Dear Sam,

This is REALLY the only way to reach you — a letter (I hope). Anyway, this is to remind you that our opening day of the 1977 season is set for Saturday, June 4 at Catholic High. We are having, of course, brief opening day ceremonies which are expected to begin around 9:00 A.M. and I personally am extending a —personal— invitation to you, Mrs. Coppola and your beautiful children to be present.

I am grateful that I am responsible for the new name the league directors have overwhelmingly approved which shall be known from June 4, 1977 and on. You may have already noticed it above on the newly designed letterhead we now use.   I am indeed proud and it is a very special honor to me that I can serve as the first Commissioner of the SAM COPPOLA 13-15 BASEBALL LEAGUE.

I will try with my very best ability to live up to the standards of superb sportsmanship for which your brilliant sports background speaks for and for what your ideals in all sports stand for. You made a lot of people happy last year Sam — especially the 90 kids that made up our new league. And as your close friend, I personally thank you for the special opportunity you gave me to be among your choice people when it all began.

Please make every effort possible to attend the opening day event. I realize your heavy business commitments, but without you there — it's like really having nothing at all.

I will contact you by phone in the next few days about having some of your men bringing the Scoreboard up to Catholic High and hanging it for us as you said.   Thank you again.

Yours in Sports,

DICK MOLLO

DM/lsp

THE AMERICAN - ITALIAN ASSOCIATION =13 - 15= BASEBALL LEAGUE

PLAYER • MANAGER • COACH
1976
APPRECIATION
AWARD

Presented To

Sam Coppola

In special Recognition of 'Exceptional' Service - and - Dedication to Others through Integrity, Loyalty, Leadership -and- Sportsmanship in the Finest American tradition.

October 17, 1976
Stamford, Connecticut

Award presentation in behalf of All Players, Coaching Staffs and Managers of competitive teams in the Inaugural 1976 season of the American-Italian Association Baseball League.

DMA - '76

Hilton Head and Ice Cream Circus

"Treat people as if they were what they ought to be and you help them to become what they are capable of being."
Goethe

Charles Magyar was a decade younger than Sam Coppola. He (Magyar) grew up in the nearby town of Greenwich, CT approximately a driver and a seven iron southeast of Stamford. So when Sam began throwing touchdowns for the Stamford Golden Bears, Charles was in his late teens.

"I used to attend the Golden Bears games regularly and it was no secret who was at the center of all the energy that this team generated week after week. Sam Coppola was the Johnny Unitas or the Bart Starr of the Atlantic Coast Football Conference and as such he was one of my heroes before I met him over a decade later."

Chronologically speaking while Sam was calling plays for the Golden Bears, Charles was finishing school, graduating in 1959 from Stamford High, and from the University of Bridgeport where he earned his B.S. in Electrical Engineering in 1966 and his MBA in 1968. With his college diploma in hand he ventured out into the real world and tested a variety of career options before settling very comfortably and successfully into commercial real estate.

"Naturally Stamford Tile interacted regularly with companies in the commercial real estate market which is where Sam and I first made each other's acquaintance," Charles said. But it wasn't until Sam, Millie, Charles, and his wife Rita happened to be boarding the same plane en route to

Puerto Rico that they had an opportunity to sit down and get to know one another.

The Puerto Rican Connection

"Prior to that, Sam and I were casual business acquaintances and I was of course a fan who'd watched him play football on many occasions. So, when I spotted Sam and Mille walking down the aisle of that plane I immediately stood up and shook hands with him. Then Sam introduced Millie, I introduced Rita, and we ended up swapping stories all the way to Puerto Rico," Charles said.

"During the following week we went out to dinner several times and we discovered that we had a lot of things in common. That week in Puerto Rico was the beginning of a very unique friendship between the Coppola family and the Magyar family," he added.

In the wake of that initial Puerto Rican adventure there were many more dinners and shows, drinks and good times. But one experience that really stands out in the mind of Charles Magyar was when his son Michael decided to try out for a Little League baseball team, failed to make the cut, and was really feeling down in the dumps.

Sam Befriends Charles' Son

"To be honest, Michael was a good athlete at the time, but he'd played very little baseball. Because of his success in other sports he was expecting to succeed at baseball too. When he didn't, it took the air out of his sails," Charles said.

"When Sam caught wind of it, he took Mike aside and started working with him on his hitting, fielding, and throwing. And to have a superman like Sam Coppola showing confidence, and telling you that you have what it takes if you only work on these things – well that's all it took to blow all the wind back in Mike's sails."

It's often been said that the highest compliment anyone can pay a parent is to fully appreciate their kids. "Sam always had a special feeling for the underdog," said Charles. "And when he learned that Mike had missed the cut and was feeling down, he immediately empathized and decided to take action. And of all the memories I have of our friendship over the years that one's really hard to beat. And it was so typical of Sam. The guy always had a heart as big as a watermelon, and the kids he interacted with all loved him."

The Undeniable Influence of JoJo

So, where did all that underdog empathy come from? Charles speculates that Sam was heavily influenced by his older brother JoJo.

"Having a family member who was as seriously challenged as JoJo," said Charles, "colored almost every step that Sam Coppola took in life. It created a strong empathy for the underdog that's pretty hard to duplicate otherwise. And to find that quality in an athletically gifted guy like Sam is almost unheard of," he added.

The NFL in 1982
San Francisco defeated Cincinnati 26-21 in Super Bowl XVI at the Pontiac Silverdome, in the first Super Bowl held in the North, January 24. The CBS telecast achieved the highest rating of any televised sports event ever, 49.1 with a 73.0 share. The game was viewed by a record 110.2 million fans. CBS Radio reported a record 14 million listeners for the game.

Sam and Charles got to know each other well enough that they became occasional business partners, buying and selling properties and making some money together. In the summer of 1980 Charles invited Sam to go to Hilton Head in South Carolina to play a little golf.

"I was a golfer but Sam was not, so I figured that despite all his natural athletic gifts I'd be able to keep up with him on the golf course," Charles said. "So we took this trip to Hilton Head and in between golf rounds we checked out the local real estate market. It was so much more affordable than the New York area that Sam and I bought several pieces of property. Sam just fell in love with Hilton Head."

Moving to Hilton Head

Upon returning, Sam told Millie all about what he'd seen and experienced at Hilton Head. After several days of discussion they announced that the Coppola family was going to move to Hilton Head in order to set up residence. As Sam already knew, Millie was also an adventurer at heart.

"However, several years before that event Sam had come up with a restaurant franchising idea that he called Burger Circus," said Charles. "This was long before Ronald McDonald or Wendy's, and he had all the details worked out right down to the striped uniforms."

With help of a couple of his Stamford Tile guys Sam constructed a model of what a Burger Circus would look like, complete with fancy circus like tiles. It was so well done that Charles invested some money, and they both made the venture capitalist rounds trying to raise capital. But for a variety of reasons Burger Circus was never consummated.

Charles and Sam

Ice Cream Circus

"But when Sam moved to Hilton Head he had to choose between finding a coaching job as Dick Mollo had encouraged, and a gainful business opportunity. He decided to launch a restaurant called Ice Cream Circus that was a cut down edition of his Burger Circus concept. For four years Sam, Millie, and the kids worked dawn to dusk and they had that place hitting on all cylinders," said Charles.

After four years, with his mom getting worse, JoJo and Stamford Tile both needing his attention, Sam finally decided he had to sell Ice Cream Circus - for a healthy profit - and he moved his family back home to Stamford.

"Ice Cream Circus was so typical of Sam," said Charles. "He was always a big thinker and he could see tendencies on the horizon that others were unable to see. He was also able to take a big idea, like Burger Circus and cut it down into something that he could manage on his own. Ice Cream Circus was a great example of that unique ability."

In the mid 80's shortly after Sam and family had returned from their four year Hilton Head adventure, Charles bought an apartment complex that included a bar called Manley's. "One of the reasons I bought the place was for my brother in law, Joe Pace, who was a world class chef. We redecorated and Sam and his brother Mike tiled all the bathrooms and the kitchen. It was slick," said Charles.

From Manley's to Paces

He changed the name from Manley's to Paces – in deference to his brother in law. They had a 10' X 10' dance floor and they played Frank Sinatra and Tony Bennett music expecting to cater to a Sinatra/Bennett like crowd.

"Then one day for kicks I went out and bought a big mirror ball, dangled it from the ceiling disco style, and we began attracting a younger crowd," said Charles. "My wife, who's a very attractive woman in her own right, had some very attractive friends who we went out of our way to invite."

"We increased the cover charge from two bits to two bucks, expanded from 1000 square feet to 5000 square feet, and before we knew it Paces became the hottest disco place in the area. We had lines so long that I'd occasionally walk outside and suggest a place down the road. But Paces was simply the place to be back then."

The NFL in 1984
The Colts relocated to Indianapolis, March 28. Their new home became the Hoosier Dome. The owners awarded two Super Bowl sites at their May 23-25 meetings: Super Bowl XXI, to be played on January 25, 1987, to the Rose Bowl in Pasadena; and Super Bowl XXII, to be played on January 31, 1988, to San Diego Jack Murphy Stadium. The New York Jets moved their home games to Giants Stadium in East Rutherford, New Jersey.

After one particularly good business cycle Charles suggested that he and Sam take a guy's only golf weekend in Puerto Rico. To sweeten the pot Charles informed Sam that he'd pay for the travel and accommodations if Sam would tend to the food and tips…a deal that was hard to refuse.

Puerto Rican Golf All Over Again

At that moment though, Sam had a lot on his plate with Stamford Tile, The House of Tile, real estate ventures, not to mention Millie, the kids, his mom and JoJo. So he told Charles he'd be unable to make it. Then at the very last minute Sam changed his mind and the trip was back on.

Both quickly packed their bags including their clubs, and while the baggage was being loaded on the plane Charles jokingly told his friend that he noticed his own clubs but not Sam's. Thinking nothing of it until they reached Puerto Rico the guys discovered that the airlines had indeed lost Sam's clubs and to his dismay, he had to rent a set.

"We stayed at the Dorado Beach Country Club where Chi Chi Rodriguez was the pro at the time. It was actually a PGA tournament stop in those days," Charles said. "We played a lot of golf, ate a lot of great food, and Sam tipped so heavily that I kidded him about spending more on tips than I spent on travel and lodging."

After a week they flew back into JFK sporting dark tans. Sam was dressed in an all white open collared suit, and Charles wore shorts and a beach comber's shirt.

"I was exhausted so I ask Sam if he'd mind shutting Paces down for me that evening. I warned him that we occasionally had rough necks at the door. That's when I found out that Sam had boxed in a previous life. He assured me that even in his white suit, he could take care of any problems. "

A Discrepancy in the Numbers

Several weeks later Charles was complaining to Sam over the fact that he was collecting less money at the door than he'd expected. Sam suggested that Charles experiment by letting him supervise the door for a couple of evenings.

"I said I was up for it if he was. As the result Sam collected two or three times as much at the door that evening as we'd ever collected before. We concluded the door guy was skimming off the top, so Sam continued collecting for a year before the demands of his own businesses put an end to it," said Charles. "Integrity was Sam's middle name."

The NFL in 1986
Chicago defeated New England 46-10 in Super Bowl XX at the Louisiana Superdome, January 26. The Patriots had earned the right to play the Bears by becoming the first wild-card team to win three consecutive games on the road. Super Bowl XX was televised to 59 foreign countries and beamed via satellite to the QE II. An estimated 300 million Chinese viewed a tape delay of the game in March.

The American Way

According to Charles, there was another venture that helps paint a portrait of Sam Coppola. "Sam had twenty five or thirty guys working for him at Stamford Tile. And like a lot of guys who labor for a living, a number of Sam's employees were unable to get credit or were being charged high rates," Charles said. "That realization caused Sam's underdog to start barking like crazy. Before long he'd decided to form a new credit card company called The American Way, designed specifically to help working people get credit."

Sam, President and Joe Zezima, VP American Way

Sam started by generating a business plan. He invested a good chunk of money himself. He recruited other investors. Rita helped him find office space. He and his staff recruited

Stamford area merchants to participate, and the American Way grew successfully for approximately two years.

"In the end though," Charles said, "Sam was trying to compete against the big bankers, and when push came to shove he simply lacked the financial muscle to compete in that league. It's one of the few times in Sam's life when his passes fell short of their target."

Nevertheless, the American Way credit card venture is another example of Sam Coppola standing up for JoJo, for the proverbial underdog, for kids in Stamford who were being denied a chance to play baseball, for people who were being denied various kinds of opportunities. That was repugnant to Sam and when he saw it, and he tried to correct it.

It's a Wonderful Life

"When I look back on three decades of friendship with Sam, the most amazing thing to me is his innate humility. The only reason I knew about his football prowess is because I attended the Golden Bears games. It wasn't because he talked about it to anyone. Like Jimmy Stewart in the movie *It's a Wonderful Life*, if you were to pull Sam Coppola out of the mix, the fortunes of everyone he's touched over the years would change for the worse. I've always been proud to call Sam a friend," said Charles.

Coppola Marble and Granite

"Genius is one percent inspiration and ninety-nine percent perspiration." **Thomas Alva Edison**

There are those who preach the doctrine of working smart over and above the doctrine of working hard. Such an interpretation implies that working smart minimizes or even eliminates the need to work hard.

But in the world of Sam Coppola, it's not enough just to work smart. In order to maximize the possibility of reaching all your goals, you're obligated to use all the tools in your toolbox, including the opportunity to apply yourself and work hard at those things that are important to you.

In Sam's words, "I've always thought that knowing how to apply yourself and work hard is one very important form of intelligence. I'm sure I inherited that from my parents who were both hard workers. I've known one too many people who earned their college degrees and then thought the world owed them a living. Needless to say, I always felt those people were selling themselves short."

Sam, however, doesn't suggest that good fortune plays no role in success. Undoubtedly, it does. "I've never argued with being lucky," he said. "But if you put all your eggs in the good fortune basket, you reduce your odds of success dramatically. You inadvertently shoot yourself in the foot."

Good Luck is When...

Sam was always a strong proponent of the old adage that says, *good luck is when preparation meets opportunity.* "In other words, if I work hard and prepare myself, I'll be ready when opportunity comes knocking at my door. That's the way I played sports. That's the way I approached business. And that's the way I've lived my life," he added.

"There are very few guarantees in life," he said. "But this much I will guarantee. You shortchange yourself when you fail to use the tools and the talents that Mother Nature and the Good Lord have given to you," said Sam.

For example, in the wake of a successful career in athletics, and a number of successful business experiences, Sam fell in love with Hilton Head South Carolina. In fact he was so intrigued by Hilton Head that he decided to move his entire family in order for them to enjoy all the things that this magical place had to offer.

When he moved, Sam had made a significant amount of money, especially in the real estate side of things, so he really didn't have to go to work immediately. He took his time and thought about the possibilities before finally deciding that he wanted to launch a small business instead of going into coaching as his good friend Dick Mollo had encouraged him to do.

> **The NFL in 1987**
> *A special payment program was adopted to benefit nearly 1,000 former NFL players who participated in the League before the current Bert Bell NFL Pension Plan was created and made retroactive to the 1959 season. Players covered by the new program spent at least five years in the League and played all or part of their career prior to 1959. Each vested player would receive $60 per month for year of service in the League for life. Over 400 former NFL players from the pre-1959 era received their first payments from NFL owners, July 1.*

From Burger Circus to...

With one decision made, he scoured Hilton Head for a good location and he finally ran across a brand new mall that had opened up in the best part of town. He met with the mall manager and started negotiations on a 4000 square foot space where he wanted to set up something like the Burger Circus idea that he'd envisioned several years before.

The Mall Manager, however, informed Sam that another store owned the rights to hamburgers in the mall and that he'd have to try something else. So instead of burgers Sam decided he'd focus on ice cream.

He called the local Sealtest rep where he learned that the odds of succeeding with ice cream alone were lower than low and that he had to add something else to the mix if he was going to come out in the black on his investment. Sam appreciated the thoughtful advice and moved accordingly.

"I got in touch with the Mall Manager and asked if we could add hot dogs and meatball wedges to our ice cream menu. He said that was fine. As long as we stayed away from hamburgers we were good to go," said Sam.

Ice Cream Circus

So Sam officially launched Ice Cream Circus in the fall of 1982 and for four straight years he and Millie worked their tails off. "The kids were in school, but I was there early and stayed late seven days a week," said Sam. "Sometimes I swear it felt like eight days. We actually ate on the premises about ninety percent of the time."

Sam manned the grill, while Millie, Sam Jr., and Tommy (after school) covered the rest of the bases. Twice a month Sam would stay late in order to clean top to bottom and make sure the whole place sparkled.

"Ice Cream Circus was always so clean that we had zero complaints from the local authorities. In fact we'd go out of our way to invite the inspectors in to check us out because we knew that when you're in the restaurant business, cleanliness is next to godliness" Sam said. "Clean was our middle name, our reputation."

Millie, Sam and the kids all wore striped circus jackets which gave the new place a roaring 20's look and a lot of color. After the first year Sam decided to add video games to the mix starting with Pac Man, Donkey Kong, and Defenders. This added revenue to the already successful enterprise.

"The video games worked out so well that I added more and more of them," Sam said. "Within a year we were up to ten, and during the tourist season Ice Cream Circus was hitting on all cylinders."

After four years of this challenging schedule the Coppola's decided to look into selling the business. "At the same time Ma was also deteriorating back in Stamford and she really needed help with JoJo. So with all that going on, I decided this was the right time to sell the business," Sam said.

He contacted a couple real estate agents and within a month he found a local lawyer who was interested in buying the place outright. Sam and the lawyer negotiated the deal and suddenly members of the Coppola family found themselves headed back home to Stamford.

Working Smart and Hard

Thinking back on his four years in Hilton Head Sam said, "We did everything we could think of to work smart, but that certainly didn't eliminate the working hard part of the experience. If we had failed to add all the sweat equity, Ice Cream Circus could easily have fallen on its face. We all decided right up front that failure was unacceptable and we were going to do everything possible to insure success. That means we all worked smart and hard," Sam said.

Back Home Again in Stamford

Upon their return to Stamford, Sam rented a house for the family and he took up again where he'd left off with his mom and JoJo. In 1991, because of her deterioration, Sam had to move his mother to a nursing home, and JoJo moved in with Sam and Millie who both made sure that BroJo was getting all the care and attention he needed in order to live the life that they wanted him to be able to live.

"After we'd arranged for Ma to be in the nursing home, I used to take JoJo to visit her twice a month without fail. The facility was fifty miles from our place and Jo loved to take rides in the car. The faster I drove the better he liked it, and I tried to accommodate him up to a point," Sam said. "That trip put a smile on Jo's face every time we made it."

While Sam and family were living in Hilton Head, Mike had sold the House of Tile and had downsized Stamford Tile in order to make it more manageable. Sam was financially independent again when he and Millie got back to Stamford, so in conjunction with tending to his mom and JoJo, he kept his eye peeled for new business opportunities.

The NFL in 1988
Washington defeated Denver 42-10 in Super Bowl XXII to earn its second victory this decade in the NFL Championship Game. The game, played for the first time in San Diego Jack Murphy Stadium, drew a sellout crowd of 73,302. According to A.C. Nielsen figures, the ABC broadcast of the game was viewed in the U.S. on television by 115 million people. The game was seen live or on tape in 60 foreign countries, including the People's Republic of China, and CBS's radio broadcast of the game was heard by 13.7 million people.

In early 1987 Sam noticed that marble and granite were becoming more and more popular in upscale homes and in commercial construction as well. He researched this trend for several months before spotting a three day trade show that was scheduled to be held in Dallas, TX. He asked Sam Jr. (Tom was already busy with his own tiling venture) if he wanted to check it out and Jr. said that he was up for it.

Arriving in Dallas, Sam Jr. attended the mechanically oriented workshops, while Sam Sr. attended the marketing and finance oriented workshops. In the evenings after dinner they convened in the hotel room, pulled out their notes and began to combine their respective findings.

Coppola Marble and Granite

"On the flight home we decided to go into the marble and granite business," Sam said. "Within a few days of returning, I ordered one large cutting and polishing machine specifically designed for marble and granite. That one piece of equipment alone cost $70,000 dollars," Sam said.

"Following that I placed another order for approximately $20,000 worth of marble and granite which came from various corners of the globe. Simultaneously I found a 17,000 square foot warehouse space in an industrial park that was big enough to house production, administration, and a third of the place could be used as a showroom for walk-in customers," he said.

Sam also found another space located on Interstate One in Westport, CT that gave him a sales office and a second showroom which doubled his walk-in exposure and expanded his business opportunity."

Sam leased both places and hired local carpenters to build model bathrooms and kitchens. He also contracted with his son Tommy to do all the tile work.

"They did an unbelievable job and when we finally had our Grand Opening people were astounded with everything they saw," Sam said. "As they say, you don't get a second chance to make a first impression. Well, our first impressions were blowing people right out of the ball park."

The Fifty-Fifty Rule

One of the foundations Sam established right out of the gate was that they were going to operate in the black and minimize the receivables by establishing a policy of getting fifty percent up front with the order, and when the job was finished he collected the other fifty percent on the spot.

"We were located in a fairly affluent part of the state," Sam said. "And we were targeting upscale buyers who were looking to make their bathrooms and their kitchens special, out of the ordinary. Our feeling was that anyone who was unwilling to abide by our fifty-fifty rule probably was not the customer we were targeting anyway."

Did they lose a few sales over this fifty-fifty policy? Sure they did. On the other hand, by expecting customers to use their own credit, Sam eliminated receivables and all the headaches that follow in the wake. This strategy allowed him to take advantage of manufacturer's discounts, which in turn kept his prices competitive and his profit margins healthy.

"As you can imagine, we'd been burned a few times at Stamford Tile by doing jobs on credit and having customers who were slow or no pay," Sam said. "That kind of thing can get costly if you're not careful, and it was a trap that Sam Jr. and I were going to avoid in this new venture."

Millie Triples the Numbers

With stellar work habits and solid financial policies in place, Coppola Marble and Granite had an excellent first year of business. "I hired a manager named Joe to oversee the Westport store and he did a good job," said Sam.

"But after the first year he became a little unhappy with us and we were feeling the same way about him so he resigned and Millie took over the reins. Petrina came in to help out on Saturdays, and between the two of them they tripled our revenues as well as our profits in year two by virtue of the relationships they naturally developed with customers."

In the meantime Sam Jr. and his crew were supporting the sales by cutting, crafting, and polishing exquisite marble and granite works of art that were being installed in kitchens and bathrooms all around the area. "We were attracting customers from a hundred miles away who came just to see what beautiful hand crafted marble and granite could do for a kitchen or a bathroom," said Sam.

Sam also took advantage of the construction contacts that he'd developed over the years in order to attract commercial jobs. "I'd spent so many years with Stamford Tile that I knew lots of contractors who were building new homes and office buildings. So we had ample opportunity to bid on commercial jobs that added to our business as well," said Sam. "But our primary focus was still residential."

Alison Redlich/Staff photo

Albert Torre Jr., right, polishes the inside of a marble sink and countertop while Tom Jacobellis buffs a slab of marble at Coppola Marble & Granite Inc. in Stamford.

Leaving no stone unfinished

Family-owned marble, granite company keeps up with growing demand

By Tom Giordano
Assistant Business Editor

When Sam Coppola describes the "beauty" of a piece of marble, you might think he was a gemologist describing the brilliance of a flawless diamond.

Coppola takes his work seriously. And at 69, the lifelong Stamford resident still maintains a daily schedule at the family business that was started by his now-deceased father, Michael, in 1927.

Back then it was called Stamford Tile Co. Today it's known as Coppola Marble & Granite Inc. Until 1992, the company dealt primarily in ceramics, "but the demand for marble was growing considerably," said Coppola. "So turning more and more to marble and granite was the logical thing to do to grow the business and meet customer demand."

And grow the business did. When Coppola first joined the family-owned business in 1955 shortly after a two-year stint with the U.S. Marines, and through 1961, the firm was grossing about $200,000 a year. Today, it brings in $3 million a year, Coppola said.

"It wasn't that long ago that only the wealthy could afford to have marble throughout the home," Coppola said. "Now, anyone can afford it."

He explained that prices for formica and corian, an acrylic, rose faster than the price of marble "until there was only about a 4 percent difference in cost to have something made with marble."

Coppola, who has a degree in business from Fordham University, was attached to personnel and played sports in the military. He was an ex-athlete who loved sports, having played semi-professional football with the now-defunct Stamford Golden Bears as their quarterback.

Coppola Marble fashions pieces for vanities, bathrooms, kitchen countertops and other uses, from marble and granite exported to the U.S. from all over the world.

The company's manufacturing is done at a leased 17,000-square-foot facility at 64 Research Drive, which also houses its administrative offices, warehouse and showroom. Coppola Marble also has a sales office and showroom in Westport, which is operated by Coppola's wife, Mildred. Cop-

Please see MARBLE, Page A15

In 1993 Sam's mother passed away and after the wake he, Millie, Petrina, and JoJo moved into his mom's home where they all lived for two years before Charles Magyar spotted another home for sale located on West Trail Road in Stamford that he thought Sam and Millie might be interested in buying.

"This was a good size place," Sam said, "with a big two car garage sitting directly beneath the house that I thought had potential for becoming apartments for JoJo and Petrina, who were both still living with us at that time. We bought it, invested another $25,000, and added a brand new two car garage on the side of the house in order to make it fit our needs. For eight years it served as our family home, allowed us all to give maximum attention to JoJo, and it was a great nest for the family as well."

So even while the business was growing like crazy, a day never passed without Sam spending quality time with JoJo. Sam made sure that Jo got showered several times a week, and Millie's cooking – especially the deserts - made JoJo feel like a king.

Time to Sell Another Business

Finally after 12 more years of living in overdrive, Sam decided the time had finally come for him to consider kicking back and relaxing a little. He talked with Millie and Sam Jr., and everyone agreed that they should look into the possibility of selling the business.

"The economy seemed to be in great shape. This was prior to the 911 attack on the World Trade Building so generally speaking people had jobs and money, and it just felt like the time was right for selling the business. When we went looking for a buyer one of our managers expressed and interest, so we sat down with him, negotiated terms and we sold Coppola Marble and Granite in 1999," said Sam.

Guarding His Time

From that point on Sam made it his business to guard his time in such a way that he would be able to concentrate on the things that were most important to him, meaning Millie, the kids, and of course, JoJo.

> **The NFL in 1993**
> *The Dallas Cowboys defeated the Buffalo Bills 52-17 in Super Bowl XXVII to capture their first NFL title since 1978. The game was played before a crowd of 98,374 at the Rose Bowl in Pasadena, California. The NBC broadcast of the game was the most watched program in television history and was seen by 133,400,000 people in the United States.*

With regard to the kids, Sam and Millie made sure that each one had access to the resources necessary to start their own respective business enterprises. Sam Jr. came out in good shape as the result of selling Coppola Marble and Granite. Tommy chose to go into his own tiling business. And Petrina and her husband Marco started a staffing enterprise which they own and operate to this day.

JoJo's Final Years

With regard to JoJo, he lived with Sam and Millie up until 2001. He finally deteriorated to the point that they could no longer cope with Jo's needs, so Sam decided it was time to move Jo into a nursing home (a mile and a half away) that was equipped to handle these kinds of challenges for the last two years of his life. Nevertheless, Sam made it a point to visit Jo every single day of the week, while Petrina and Millie made it several times each month.

"JoJo was such an important part of our family for as far back as I can remember," Sam said. "It got to the point that I felt like he was my son. And the kids loved him as well, especially Petrina who had a unique relationship with her Uncle Jo. They appreciated each other in a way that's kind of hard to describe. But if you watched them interact it was undeniable," said Sam.

So whether it was football or baseball, business or the family Sam did his best to incorporate solid work habits and intelligent decisions with an eye towards winning the game.

The NFL in 1999
Walter Payton, the NFL's all-time leading rusher, died of liver cancer at the age of 45. Payton played for the Chicago Bears from 1975-1987 and rushed for an NFL-record 16,726 yards, November 1. Former NFL Commissioner Pete Rozelle, who guided a still-developing league to its position today as America's most popular sport, was named by The Sporting News as the most powerful person in sports in the 20th Century, December 15.

Wise Words From Ben Hogan

"I read one time that golfing great Ben Hogan claimed that his winning strategy was threefold. *First he said he'd try and intimidate his opponent,*" said Sam. "*If that didn't work then he'd try and outsmart his opponent. And if the first two didn't work, he'd just plain outwork 'em.* In our case, we never intimidated anyone. But we did try to make intelligent decisions, and we always worked our tails off," said Sam. "So the last part of Hogan's quote I could always identify with."

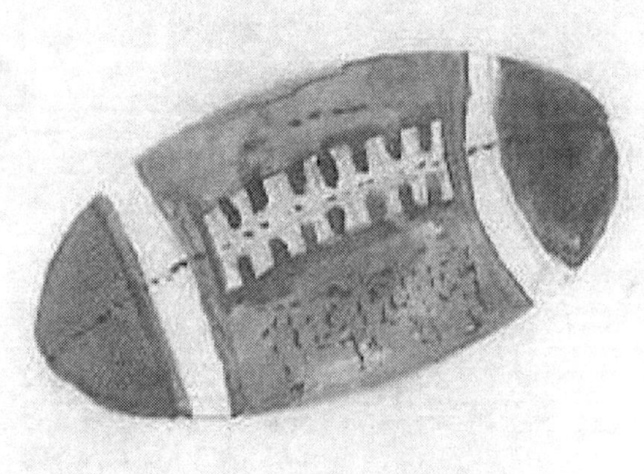

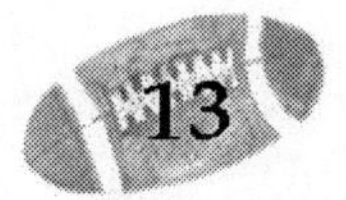

13

Sam's Hall of Fame and Sam's Hall of Shame

*"For when the One Great Scorer comes
To write against your name,
He marks not that you won or lost –
But how you played the Game."*
Grantland Rice

By virtue of being born into an Italian American family in 1930 Sam was raised Catholic. And to this day Sam still considers himself an active member of the Catholic Church.

But as we know by now, Sam was also a player of football and baseball, and as such his practical, concrete, hands-on reference to concepts like right and wrong, good and bad, fair and unfair, just and unjust, came more from sports than from religion.

In both baseball and football there are rules and regulations, limitations and restrictions that are specifically designed to define and to distinguish one game from another, and to make the actions within it meaningful. So tackling for example, in football is a very important skill, but tackling in baseball or basketball is strictly prohibited.

In football you'd be cheered by the crowd for a good tackle. In baseball or basketball a tackle would be boo'd by the crowd, and would result in a penalty, a fine, and possibly a complete ejection from the game.

In other words, take the rules and regulations away and it's impossible to distinguish football apart from baseball or basketball. Rules and regulations simultaneously create meaningful freedom, and they prevent chaos.

Fair and Balanced

Not only that, but the rules and regulations of a game must be applied equally to all participants in order to maintain any sense of fairness, justice, and meaning. If the ref favors one team over another team, the results (team A is better or worse than team B) of the game are suddenly rendered unfair and therefore, meaningless.

Players who willfully take unfair advantage over an opponent are cheating and are also guilty of rendering the results of the game meaningless. A level playing field is an underlying presumption for all sports and maintaining it through fair and just treatment of all participants is a sporting moral imperative that borders on sacredness.

In that light let's explore *Sam's Hall of Fame*, a group made up of people who Sam admires and looks up to because they reflect the way he values sport. After that we'll explore *Sam's Hall of Shame*, a group made up of people who Sam does not admire or look up to because they fail to reflect the way he values sport.

Sam's Hall of Fame: Kurt Warner

Sam has a soft spot in his heart for many football players including the late, great Johnny Unitas (of the Baltimore Colts, 1956 to 1974) who began his career playing semi-pro football (the Bloomfield Rams for $6 a game), and wound up as one of the most revered quarterbacks to ever play the game. He also thinks highly of Joe Montana and Jerry Rice, both formerly of the San Francisco 49'ers.

But it won't surprise you to learn that Sam's favorite football player is a quarterback. Kurt Warner who recently retired from the Arizona Cardinals and who'd previously played with the New York Giants and the St. Louis Rams sits at the very top of Sam's football totem pole.

"I just loved the entire Kurt Warner story," said Sam. "He attended a small college, Northern Iowa University and

was not drafted by the NFL. But he didn't give up on his dreams either. After trying out with several NFL teams including the Green Bay Packers when Brett Favre first arrived, Kurt went to Europe and played football."

"He returned to the states and played in the Arena League for a couple of years, and was bagging groceries in his home town of Cedar Rapids, IA before the St. Louis Rams called him in to back up starter Trent Green. Green got hurt, Warner stepped in and was suddenly directing traffic for a team that John Madden called The Greatest Show on Turf."

"He's a strong family man who's proud of his wife and kids. In his spare time he helps kids all over Arizona and his home state of Iowa. If there's ever been a better Cinderella story in the NFL I've missed it," said Sam. "That's why Kurt Warner's my favorite football player of all time," he added.

Ray Allen

In basketball, former University of Connecticut super star guard Ray Allen occupies Sam's top position. "I started watching him during his college days at The University of Connecticut." Sam said. "And he was always the guy who spoke softly and carried the big stick – in the form of a unique ability to connect from three point range."

"I've never seen Allen trash talking anyone. Now I'm not saying that he couldn't be provoked, but it would take a lot for anyone to get this guy upset. He's always cool whether he's winning or losing. I've never seen Ray Allen acting like anything less than a complete gentleman's gentleman. In a game where the egos are as big as the incredibly inflated salaries, Allen shows that success doesn't have to go to your head. He's also a proud husband and dad. I'll take Ray Allen and Kurt Warner on my team every day of the week," Sam said.

Big Mike

In baseball Sam always loved the Yankee Clipper Joe DiMaggio who not only (still) owns the Major League's record of hitting safely in 56 consecutive games, but he also served as the Grand Marshall of a Sam Coppola Baseball League event. Sam's also a big Derick Jeter fan, along with Jackie Robinson (who lived in Stamford during his Dodger days) and Pete Rose – he's paid his dues and now deserves a place in the MLB hall of fame.

However, Sam's favorite baseball player of all times is his brother Mike. "Mike was a natural," said Sam. "He was two inches taller than me, about 15 lbs heavier. He was strong as an ox, hit for average, and could hit a ball further than any human I've ever seen. He was also an excellent outfielder but today they'd play Mike at first base in order to extend his career at the plate. If he'd stayed in baseball he'd be well known in all baseball circles today. Anyway, Mike is my hero of heroes when it comes to baseball," said Sam.

BROTHER ACT in the sports world, Mike and Sam Coppola of Stamford enter into "big-time" professional sports this year, as Sam, left, joins the Green Bay Packers football team, and Mike, right, steps into Class A Sally League play with the Jacksonville Baseball Club.

Coppola Brothers Seek Spot in Big-Time Sports Picture

Ron Gorton, right, exchanges stories with Jack Hagan during the Stamford Old Timers dinner in December 1998. Gorton, a former Stamford High athlete who went on to play football at Villanova University and minor league baseball, died recently in Florida. He was 69. Dugan and Gorton were teammates on the 1950 Stamford High state football champions. Hagan also coached at Stamford High.

Gorton led a full and storied life

Ronnie Gorton

One of Sam's unsung sporting heroes was an old friend named Ronnie Gorton who became a very successful movie director. But Sam knew him as a marvelous athlete and wrote the following letter when Ronnie passed away in 2002.

Dear Gorton family,

I read in the Stamford Advocate about the passing of Ronnie –who was a real friend of mine. We go back many years – which I'd like to share with you at this time.

I met Ronnie when he was 13 years old. I was 16 at the time. We met at Woodside Park which is now Scalzi Park, and I was working out with a couple of football players who introduced me to a young and talented passer named Ronnie Gorton. Ronnie and I took turns throwing the football (at that time I was quarterbacking at St. Basil) and he really impressed me – to the point that I said "this kid is a natural."

Many years passed by and I had played at Fordham and in the Marine Corps and I'd heard that Ronnie quarterbacked at Villanova University. After the Marines I returned home to Stamford and played quarterback with the Stamford Golden Bears.

A couple years later I got a call from Ronnie about the semi pro baseball team I was sponsoring and playing for, the Stamford Tilers. He said he was between films, returning to Stamford, and wanted to play for my team. I said ok. It was amazing that Ronnie hadn't picked up a ball for a long time and he came to Barrett Field and played as if he'd been playing every day. What an athlete.

I started my second year with the Golden Bears and during our first practice I was told that Ronnie Gorton was joining our team to compete for the quarterbacking job. So now I was going to compete against the kid that I thought so highly of – but I loved the idea of competition.

But we never heard from Ronnie until we read in the paper that he'd joined the Port Chester Alfonso's team – which we were scheduled to play in two weeks. We competed and the Golden Bears won, but Ronnie and I met after the game and I asked what happened? You were supposed to join our club. He said "I'm not going to compete against someone who's my friend and mentor."

This was Ronnie – a sincere, talented, true friend. By the way he was great in that game, and I can only wonder how good he'd have been if he'd practiced, worked out and knew the system. What a talent for a guy who hadn't picked up a football for so long!

Ronnie and I met again at the Italian Center when I was one of the old timers being honored in February of 1992. He had a great sense of humor and he was a guy who I just loved to be around.

I will always wonder what would have happened if he'd pursued football or baseball full time. I think he'd have made it big in either sport. Sorry I'm unable to make the memorial service, but I wanted to express how much of a man Ronnie Gorton was. Please express my sincere condolences to all the family.

We lost a great guy.

Sincerely,
Sam Coppola

Old Blue Eyes

Of course Sam had a full life and plenty of interests outside of sports. For example, Sam was a connoisseur of music and his favorite singer was always "old blue eyes" himself, Frank Sinatra.

"Sinatra was not only the most popular singer of my era, but he was a friend of Dick Mollo who was my partner in the Sam Coppola Baseball League. Dick was with Frank on one occasion and asked him to write a note in support of our baseball league. Dick pulled out a photograph and Frank signed it on the spot. Ever since then, Sinatra has been my favorite singer. Not only that but my favorite song of all times is Sinatra's *My Way*. I always loved the lyrics to that song."

Sam at the Movies

Sam's favorite movies include Godfather I, Godfather II, Good Fellows, Rocky, and The Gladiator. "My favorite actors are Robert De Niro, Marlon Brando, Susan Hayward, and Marlene Dietrich," said Sam. "I liked the gangster movies and I was always rooting for the underdog. When the underdog won, I won," he added. "Me and JoJo."

Sam's Favorite Writers

Sam's favorite writers just happened to be sports writers including Mel Allen and Howard Cosell. "I loved Mel Allen and the Friday Night Fights, brought to you by White Owl Cigars and Gillette Blue Blades. Throw in Rocky Marciano, Ezzard Charles, Jersey Joe Walcott, Archie Moore, Ingemar Johannson, Rocky Graziano, and Floyd Patterson and The Friday Night Fights were as big as The Honeymooners and I Love Lucy."

"Cosell of course took that whole thing to a new level with Cassius Clay/Muhammad Ali and Broadway Joe Namath. But those were my two favorite sports writers and as Millie would say, when I read, I'm reading about sports."

Sam's Favorite TV Shows

Speaking of the Honeymooners, Sam's favorite TV shows other than Friday Night Fights included Jackie Gleason and the Honeymooners, as well as Lucile Ball in I Love Lucy. "Back then I didn't have much time for TV but when I had a chance to sit down with JoJo and tune in I always loved Ralph and his wife Alice, Norton and his wife Trixie. I swear I had friends who behaved the same way they did."

"The other show was I Love Lucy. If I even think about the scene when Lucy and Ethyl are working on the chocolate candy assembly line I start laughing out loud. If there was ever a wackier comedian than Lucile Ball I never saw her. And of course JoJo had me watching Roy Rogers and the Three Stooges which were his favorites. I don't think they make shows like those any more, and I wish they did," Sam said with a little nostalgia in his voice.

"I watch more TV these days than I ever did because I'm retired and I've become a fan of Jeopardy and Who Wants to be a Millionaire," Sam said. "But I'd take The Honeymooners or I Love Lucy over anything I see today."

To this list of heroes I'd like to add all the people that I talked about in the preceding chapters, and I'm sure I've overlooked some. But if they hadn't been extremely influential in my life I wouldn't have mentioned them, whether it was on the field or off the field.

And at this point I want to add my own kids Sam Jr., Tommy, and Petrina who are all unique and wonderful people in their own right. I love and respect them all more than I can say."

"And while I'm at it, I want to mention my wonderful grandkids Sam III and Ryan, who are Sammy's kids. Justin is Petrina's, and Tom Jr., Zachery, and Karly are Tommy's kids. Every time I look at any one of them I know how much Millie and I have been blessed. They're all my heroes."

Business, Politics, and Social Entrepreneurs

In the business world Sam always admired Lee Iacocca who, with the help of a bailout, steered Chrysler Corporation out of bankruptcy back in the early 70's. As for politicians Sam likes Harry Truman and Ronald Reagan. Obviously he was an independent voter. He was a big admirer of Martin Luther King, John F. Kennedy, and Arthur Ashe the well known tennis player from Richmond, VA.

"To me these guys played the game by the rules and are the people I looked up to," said Sam. "Not that they were perfect, but in my eyes they were all good people."

Sam's Hall of Shame

Now we'll briefly mention a few people who Sam does not admire and hold in high esteem primarily because of the way they've ignored the rules and dragged the sports that he loved down into the sewer. At the top of this list are all the steroid users in professional sports whether they're in football or baseball or anywhere else.

"In the long run steroids have been proven to be very unhealthy, but in the short run the players who are willing to break the rules and use them gain an unfair advantage over the players who play the game by the rules."

Cheaters are Cheaters

"They're cheaters and they don't deserve the respect they get. Whether it's McGwire, Clemens, Bonds or A-Rod, each of these players should have an asterisk after their name forever in order to designate that they didn't respect the game and were only after the material rewards it gave to them. I also contend they should publish the entire list of steroid offenders in order to clear the names of all those baseball players who are playing by the rules."

And football is no different than baseball. "Cheaters are cheaters, and if they're willing to sacrifice the game itself for their own selfish, short term gain, I lose respect for their short-sighted self centeredness," Sam said.

By the way, business is no different than sports for Sam. "That means if the financiers on Wall Street committed the fraud they've been accused of committing, they fall into the same league as the cheaters in sports. When they take unfair advantage of others, they wreck the game for everyone except themselves. That's unadulterated greed, and I have no respect for that whether it's on or off the field," said Sam.

A Person is Reflected by His Heroes

"They say you can get to know a person by knowing who he or she looks up to, and the people in this chapter and in this book are some of the people I look up to and admire. And if that's a reflection of Sam Coppola then I guess I'll have to say I'm flattered by it. Thank you."

Why?

"Regrets, I have a few. But then again, there are a few I should probably mention." **Sam Coppola**

Flip the calendar forward through two, four, six, and eight years since Sam and Millie sold Coppola Marble and Granite, Inc., along with their home in Stamford, CT, packed their bags and moved south to Boca Raton, FL. Sam is still an early riser, and both he and Millie have a plethora of worthwhile activities with which to fill their days.

It was in the fall of 2003 when they finally got themselves settled in Boca Raton when Millie looked at Sam and said something like, "I've been cooking and grocery shopping for this family for the past forty years while you've been running the businesses, playing football and baseball, dabbling in real estate, and overseeing a kid's baseball league. Since you're a great cook and you like to grocery shop, I think the time has come for you take over those activities."

Italian Cuisine

Sam agreed and he took over the cooking and grocery shopping duties while Millie took up a hobby that she'd been wanting to take up for a long time - tennis.

"I specialize in Italian cuisine," Sam said. "The entire family has always loved lasagna, linguine, and spaghetti with meatballs. Anyone who's tasted a steak that I've grilled on the barbeque is ruined for life. When Petrina comes in town she makes her home made pizza which is always big a hit. And yes, I also do all the grocery shopping."

"In the meantime Millie has developed a pretty mean forehand, backhand, and she doesn't serve too bad either," said Sam. "Unfortunately my knees won't allow me to be her doubles partner, but I can still put a tight spiral on the football if you're interested in seeing that."

Actually, the one thing he doesn't do around the house is the landscaping. Once again, mowing aggravates the knees and that's an aggravation Sam can do without these days.

Practical Landscaping

"I have a great landscaper named Elder Silva who's originally from Brazil and we've become good friends," Sam said "He takes care of me and I take care of him when I can because he does spectacular work. I've recommended him to all my friends in the neighborhood and he's gotten lots of jobs as the result."

Since they first met, Elder has become Sam's trusted friend on all things practical. "I had a problem for example, with my swimming pool pump, so I called a pool company to come out and give me a quote. But before I accepted the quote I had Elder look it over. When he saw it he laughed out loud, got one of his guys to do the work, and charged me a third of what the other guys quoted," Sam said. "Like I said, we take care of each other."

Sam and Millie's six grandkids

Grand Parenthood

Sam and Millie also spend some time with the grand kids whenever they visit. "After we moved, Sam Jr. and his wife Jackie visited several times and decided they liked life in the warmer climate too," said Sam. "The kids, including the grandkids, love everything I throw on the barbeque. Petrina and Tommy still live in Stamford, but they get down here on the holidays. Millie and I both love grand parenthood."

Coin Collecting

In his spare time Sam has expanded on a coin collecting hobby that he's started over 30 years ago. "Now that I've retired I have time to correspond with other coin collectors around the country," he said. "I get a couple of coin collecting publications, and I attend a trade show every once in a while. I've developed some good friends that I would never have known had it not been for my coin collecting hobby," Sam said.

Wild Green Parakeets feeding in Sam and Millie's yard

For the Birds...

Sam has also developed an interest in birds and when he's at the grocery store he often buys food for the feeder in his back yard. "I do my best to have food that attracts the blue birds, robins & the wild green parakeets. But too often the squirrels drop in and run the others off. When I see those little bullies come in, I always go out and chase 'em away. But I know they get their share when I'm not around," said Sam.

The Silent Quarterback

The other thing that's soaking up Sam and Millie's time these days is riding heard on the Silent Quarterback. "This entire thing was motivated by me finally having time to sit down and to do a little introspective pondering. You know, looking back and leafing through the why's, the wherefore's, and the want if's."

The more he thought about these things, the more those thoughts entered into his conversations with friends. And the more Sam talked about these things with friends, the more people kept saying "I didn't know that about you Sam. You should write a book. It would be a great story." The more often he heard that suggestion, the more Sam thought, "Maybe they're right? My story might make for good reading? Maybe they're right?"

Thoughts Translate Into Action

Thoughts, when pondered long enough, often turn into action, especially when your name is Sam Coppola. "One afternoon I was talking to Sam Jr. about it when we both looked at each other and said, Why not?"

"Millie and I put an ad in the local newspaper looking for someone who could guide us through the process of writing and publishing a book. We generated a lot of response, made some decisions, now things are moving along right on schedule, and it's coming in precisely on budget. I feel like a movie producer who's finally bringing his pet project to the finish line," said Sam.

Nagging Questions

Since the initial motivation for the book was the nagging questions Sam had about never making it in the NFL, we should start by trying to answer that question.

"I watch Payton and Eli Manning, Brett Farve, Kurt Warner, and Tom Brady, etc and say to myself, I used to be able to do all those things they're doing now, so why did I fail to make it in the NFL? Why didn't I have the opportunity to compete with Charlie Connerly and Y.A. Tittle in the Giants' organization, with Norm Van Brocklin and the Eagles, or Billy Wade and the Bears, or Bobby Lane and the Lions?"

Several Answers

The first answer to that question is that Sam chose to take the advice of Coach Murphy who suggested he attend Fordham instead of Rutgers or Princeton, both of whom had said they wanted him to play quarterback, not another position. "The second mistake was failing to speak up once I got to Fordham and they were playing me at defensive back instead of quarterback," said Sam.

Sam (44), Zeke Bella, and Coach John Murphy

"At this stage of my life I wish I'd been more assertive like my friend Richie Conners. If I had competed and won the quarterback position in college, my odds of attracting the NFL's attention would have been much better," Sam said. "And that would have happened before I injured my knee in the service," he added. "I do have 20/20 hind sight."

So at Fordham Sam logged four years worth of experience playing defensive halfback instead of four years of experience playing quarterback. When he joined the Marines he wasn't even planning to play football until the colonel in charge of his squadron asked him to try out. When the coach asked, Sam said that he was a quarterback in college…a little white lie that translated into ten years of quarterbacking in the Atlantic Coast Football Conference.

On the other hand, once Sam began playing with the Golden Bears, leading the Atlantic Coast Conference in passing year after year, and watching as other guys successfully jumped from the semi-pro ranks into the big time, he's still troubled by the fact that he never took even one snap as an NFL quarterback.

Where Was the Shotgun?

One similar question that drops into Sam's conscience on occasion is about the shotgun formation. "When I was playing, nobody was using the shotgun, with the quarterback five yards off the center. And that gives today's players two to three more seconds to get their passes off. "

"So if I had those extra two or three seconds each play, I can't help but wonder how that would have affected my performance," Sam said. "I once posed that question to Coach Shanen and he said the shotgun wasn't part of Paul Brown's playbook, so it wasn't part of ours either."

Timing is Everything

But realistically things were so much different (including no shotgun) in the late 50's and early 60's. "I had a business to run, a family to support, and jumping into the

NFL was iffy at that point in time. So I played my heart out on the local field and had great stats, but I never pushed hard enough on the NFL door for it to open for me," said Sam. "There are days now that I wish I'd done so."

SAM COPPOLA, BULL SHORTSTOP, "COMES AROUND" ON ONE of Norm Luoni's pitches (top) and then reaches for out-stretched hand (bottom) of Milt Berty as he crosses the plate behind three El Toro runners. The action took place Tuesday in the first inning against the 11th Naval District winners; El Toro went on to win 7-5.

And There Was Baseball

When it came to baseball Sam has one other big question that haunts him to this day. "I had a legitimate 90 MPH fastball," he said. "

"But of all the years I played baseball I played lots of short-stop, plenty of third base, an occasional right field, and I did some pitching. But the right thing would have been to concentrate on pitching because that was my strongest suit."

"If I'd done that and stayed in contact with several major league teams I might have made it in baseball. But as with so many dreams, life seems to step in and circumstances determine what you do and what you don't do. I'm no exception to that rule," Sam said. "There were too many times that I was reacting to circumstances instead of proactively prioritizing the things that were most important to me. If I only knew then what seems to be so obvious now."

Sam's Father

On the other hand Sam's why's, wherefore's, and what if's aren't all about sports. The fact that he (Sam) was with his dad the night before he died, knew he was under the weather but did not insist on taking him to the hospital still lingers in Sam's memory.

"This was a guy who took pride in his health and in never having to go to the doctor for anything. But that evening he was not himself and I wished that I'd listened a little closer. Maybe I would have caught something in between the lines that would have tipped me off and I'd have insisted on taking him to the hospital. I still think about that," Sam said.

And JoJo

There are also questions about JoJo. "Having a baby is so much safer and more predictable these days. Maybe that would have made a difference in Jo's life? These days I see mentally challenged kids being mainstreamed into public schools and it's kind of astounding how much they can do when given the opportunity and when they're encouraged."

"I can't help but wonder how those kinds of experiences would have translated in JoJo's life. He might have been a Special Olympics participant. Who knows? But we didn't have Special Olympics back then, or lots of the other knowledge when it comes to educating special needs kids, so its' water over the dam, said Sam. "When it comes to JoJo however, there are a myriad of what if's."

Time Spent With Millie and the Kids

Another issue with Sam at this point in his life is, with his wall to wall schedule for all those years, did he spend enough time with his kids? "My kids are the light of my life, and thank God they're all healthy and happy with families of their own. But I still wonder if I could have been a better father if I'd cut back on my schedule, especially when they were really young and impressionable," said Sam.

"And of course Millie never complained, but she had a heavy load with our three kids and JoJo, while I was constantly out working to making ends meet, or playing ball. Would things have been different or better if I'd been less of a workaholic and I'd spent more time with my family?"

Sam and Millie today in Boca Raton, FL

But What if...

On the other hand there have been plenty of times when Sam was just plain lucky. "For example," Sam said, "what if I'd taken Tommy Uva up on his invitation to fly to Boston instead of keeping my promise to Sam Jr.? If I'd chosen to do that, I'd have never seen my kids grow up. I'd never be able to look back and contemplate the what-if's. And I certainly wouldn't be writing a book as we speak. There, but for the good lord goes I," he added.

When I Look Back

Life, when Sam looks back on it now, is a product of choices, some of them we make for ourselves, and some of them are made for us. "As much as I loved the lyrics of Sinatra's song My Way, nobody, not Frank, Kurt Warner, Ray Allen, Bruno Amato, Allen Webb, Joe DiMaggio, Babe Ruth, or Sam Coppola ever fully lived up to them," said Sam.

"Sure, I took pride in being my own boss, making my own decisions, and caring for my family. I also took pride in quarterbacking the football team, and in being on the pitching mound when I played baseball. But whether it's sports or life in general you do as much as you can do proactively to control your circumstance," Sam said.

"But inevitably there are times when circumstances turn the tables and threaten to control you. That's when you have to react instead of just act. That's when things don't always go the way you'd planned for them to go."

Faith in People, Especially Kids

"But even under the reactionary circumstances there are choices that must be made, and I'm convinced that most people try to make the best choices they can…even though the results often look otherwise. The bottom line here is that I've always believed in people, especially kids. And in reality we're all kids at heart. Some are just a little older than others."

"As Frank said in his wonderful song, *regrets, I have a few. But then again, too few to mention.* I hope you enjoyed reading this book as much as I enjoyed writing it. If you have any comments, questions, or would like to correspond, please feel free to go to my website www.silentquarterback.com and comment on anything that you'd care to comment on. I will write you back. I promise."

State of Connecticut
QUI TRANSTULIT SUSTINET
GENERAL ASSEMBLY
Official Citation
Introduced by   REPRESENTATIVE JOHN DAYNE FOX, 144TH DISTRICT
Be it hereby known to all that:
The Connecticut House
hereby offers its sincerest congratulations to:
SAM COPPOLA
in recognition of
OUTSTANDING ATHLETIC CONTRIBUTIONS AND COMMUNITY ACTIVITIES.
The entire membership extends its
very best wishes on this memorable occasion
and expresses the hope for continued success.
Given this 3RD day of FEBRUARY   19 92
at the State Capital
Hartford, Connecticut
by
Speaker of the House
Secretary of the State

SAMUEL M. COPPOLA

Born July 23, 1930 in Stamford, Connecticut. Education: Stevens School - Grammar School, Cloonan School - Middle School, St. Basils and Eastern Military - High School, Carteret - Prep School, Fordham University - College.

Sports History: Cloonan: 130 lb. city boxing champ. St. Basils: Football (quarterback), basketball, baseball, track, shotput and javelin. Pitched no hitter as a freshman. Eastern Military: Football (quarterback), Captain football team, baseball and basketball. Carteret: Captain football team and selected All State NJ and was pursued by many major colleges and offered sports scholarships. Chose Fordham because of their great schedule. Fordham: Only student to play both football and baseball. Played defensive and offensive halfback. Played third base on the baseball team. Marine Corp.: Stationed in Hawaii, 1st Lt., played football and baseball. Hit two homeruns in one game. Played quarterback on the football team and won the championship against Army, Navy with 9-1 record, Selected to Hula Bowl. Minor League Baseball: Joined brother Mike in Appalachia League 1 year. Third base.

Semi-Pro: Baseball: Twilight League. Won batting crown - batting 410. Won pitching trophy for most wins. Football: Golden Bears, quarterback Westchester Crusaders quarterback and holds league record Atlantic Coast Conference for (1) Against Pitts. Panthers threw 7 touchdown passes in 1 game (2) 26 touchdown passes 9 game season Milford Rockets quarterback. In a game against Portland Seahawks (quarterbacked by Butch Songin formerly of the NY Jets) threw 28 passes and completed 26 of which 3 were touchdown passes.

Captain of all three football teams. Organized and ran Italian American baseball league 13-15 year old boys. 150 boys on 10 teams. Name changed by State of Conn. and Dick Mollo to Sam Coppola Baseball.

Article by Sam's good friend Dick Mollo